BELOW THE SURFACE: BUILDING QUALITY SYSTEMS NOT HEROES

Chad Diggs
Dign2quality.com
March 2026

Contents

Introduction

After 20 years in manufacturing quality management, I got tired of watching the same movie play out over and over again.

A supplier ships defective parts. Production uses them anyway because they're behind schedule. Six months later, customer returns start flooding in. Engineering scrambles to identify the root cause. Quality gets blamed for "not catching it." Leadership cuts the quality budget to "improve margins."

Rinse and repeat.

I've seen this pattern destroy companies. Good companies. Companies with talented people who wanted to do the right thing but didn't have the frameworks, tools, or—most critically—the organizational buy-in to prevent problems instead of just reacting to them.

Here's what frustrated me most: the answer already exists. DFMEA, PFMEA, CAPA, COPQ, supplier quality management—these aren't new concepts. They're proven methodologies that work when implemented correctly. But they're often trapped in consultant-speak, academic papers, or $500,000 enterprise software implementations that only Fortune 500 companies can afford.

This is the practical guide I wish **someone had handed me** on day one.

You'll follow Kristina Valdez through three years of transformation at a mid-market aerospace manufacturer—from discovering $30M in hidden costs to building prevention systems that survive her departure.

The Problem with Most Quality Books

Most quality books teach you "what" to do:
- "Implement DFMEA to prevent design failures"
- "Use 8D problem-solving for root-cause analysis"
- "Develop your suppliers to improve incoming quality"

That's all true. But they don't teach you "how" to actually do it when:

- Your engineers are already underwater with design schedules
- Your budget request gets cut in half
- Your operators distrust yet another "quality initiative"
- Your suppliers push back on capability requirements
- Your new VP wants to "do things differently"

They don't show you the messy reality of organizational transformation, the politics, the resistance, the small wins that build momentum, the setbacks that test your resolve.

They give you the destination but not the journey.

Who This Book Is Written For:

You're a **Quality Manager or Engineer** who knows there's a better way than firefighting but can't get traction with leadership. This book shows you how to build the business case, secure the budget, and deliver results that prove prevention works.

You're an **Operations Leader** tired of rework, scrap, and customer complaints eating your margins. This book demonstrates how prevention investment pays 10–20× returns and creates capacity for growth without capital expenditure.

You're a **CEO or GM** who suspects quality is costing more than it should but lacks visibility into where the money goes. This book teaches you how to map "Cost of Poor Quality", track prevention ROI, and turn quality into competitive advantage.

You're a **Plant Manager** implementing lean or operational excellence and hitting quality roadblocks. This book shows how quality and operational excellence integrate—where First Pass Yield, process capability, and error-proofing fit into your continuous improvement system.

You're a **Consultant or Trainer** who wants to help clients transform quality, not just implement tools. This book provides a proven roadmap you can adapt to different industries and company sizes.

What You'll Learn

The Tools (Taught Through Story, Not Theory):

Cost of Poor Quality (COPQ): How to find quality costs hidden in other budgets—scrap buried in manufacturing overhead, warranty buried in customer service, engineering time buried in project budgets. Map your COPQ in two weeks and build the business case for prevention.

Design Failure Mode & Effects Analysis (DFMEA): How to facilitate and design a four-hour workshop that identifies failure modes before they're built into products. Rating scales explained through real examples. Risk Priority Numbers calculated naturally, not academically.

Voice of Customer (VOC): How to capture what customers actually need, not just what they specify. Site visit techniques. Interview methods. Translating requirements. Testing in actual use conditions. Preventing "meets spec but misses need" failures.

Process Capability (Cp/Cpk): How to assess whether processes can meet requirements. When Cp=1.15 predicts quality problems. How to improve capability through equipment, fixturing, or process changes. What data you need and how to interpret it.

Operator Empowerment: How to get production operators to own quality instead of deferring to inspection. Poka-yoke design principles. Psychological safety creation. Metrics that reward prevention. First Pass Yield as the key manufacturing quality metric.

Supplier Development: How to segment suppliers (Strategic/Capable/Problematic), assess capability on-site, build development plans, negotiate co-investment, and track results through scorecards. Turn vendor relationships into strategic partnerships.

8D Problem-Solving: When to use structured problem-solving versus simpler approaches. How to form cross-functional teams. Root-cause validation through testing. Corrective actions that address causes, not symptoms. Preventive actions that update systems to prevent recurrence.

Quality ROI Tracking: How to calculate prevention investment versus COPQ reduction. Prevented cost calculation (failures that didn't happen). Customer satisfaction measurement. Contract wins attributable to quality. Board presentation frameworks that prove quality is strategy, not cost.

Sustainability Systems: How to make prevention institutional through documentation, governance, talent development, and rituals. Succession planning. Leadership transition management. Cultural transformation indicators that show when prevention has become "just how we work."

The Mindset (The Harder Part)

Tools are easy. Culture change is hard.
You'll learn how to:
- "Build proof points" before asking for big investments (one project, one success, then scale)
- "Navigate politics" when prevention conflicts with short-term goals (schedule pressure, cost targets, output quotas)
- "Change metrics" so that people are rewarded for prevention, not just firefighting
- "Communicate in financial terms" leadership understands (ROI, COPQ, margin impact, strategic value)
- "Sustain through leadership changes" by making systems institutional, not personality-dependent
- "Develop your successors" so transformation continues when you leave

Free tools and templates for every methodology in this book are available at **dign2quality.com**.

Chapter 1 — The Iceberg: Seeing the True Cost of Poor Quality

Month 0: The Wake-Up Call

Kristina Valdez pulled into the Aegis Aviation parking lot at 6:42 AM and knew immediately something was wrong.

The production parking lot was full—first shift didn't start until 7:00. The loading dock had three trucks backed up waiting. Through the windows of Building 2, she could see people clustered around Line 4, arms crossed, nobody moving.

She'd seen this before. Too many times.

She grabbed her laptop and walked through the employee entrance. The smell hit her first—the acrid tang of solvent mixed with something chemical she couldn't place. Then the noise—or lack of it. The hum of production equipment was absent. Just voices, urgent and frustrated.

Mark Chen, the operations supervisor, saw her and jogged over. "Thank God you're here. We've got a situation."

"What happened?"

"Line 4. Contamination event. Whole batch of avionics housings—240 units. They went through cleaning and coating, but something was off. Coating wouldn't adhere properly. When we inspected closer, found residue on the substrate. Traced it back to the cleaning station. Wrong solvent in the tank."

Kristina felt the familiar knot in her stomach. "How wrong?"

"Acetone instead of IPA. Someone refilled from the wrong drum last night. Third shift."

"How many units affected?"

"All of them. Batch 2287-41. They're in quarantine now."

Kristina did the math in her head. Each housing was worth about $800 in material and labor at this point, 240 units. That was $192,000 sitting in quarantine. But that wasn't the real problem.

"What's the delivery date?"

Mark grimaced. "Today. Customer's expecting them at their facility by 5 PM for integration into their assembly line. This was the last shipment to complete the contract."

There it was. The *real* problem.

Kristina walked to Line 4. The housings sat on a pallet, wrapped in protective film, quarantine tags bright red. Tom Rodriguez, her quality engineer, was examining one under magnification.

"Tom, what are we looking at?"

Tom looked up. "Contamination layer between substrate and coating. The acetone left a residue that IPA would have removed. Coating's compromised. Some of it's already starting to lift."

"Can we rework them?"

"Strip the coating, re-clean with correct solvent, re-coat, re-cure, re-inspect. Four days minimum. Maybe five."

Four days. The customer would be down for four days. Kristina knew what came next.

Mark's phone rang. He looked at the screen and answered. "Yes, sir. She's right here." He handed the phone to Kristina. "VP."

She took the call. "This is Kristina."

The VP of operations got straight to it. "Mark filled me in. What's the plan?"

"We need four to five days to rework the batch properly."

Silence. Then: "Customer's not going to accept a four-day delay. They've got their own production schedule. We'll pay penalties. And we'll damage the relationship right when we're trying to win the follow-on contract."

"I understand, but the coating is compromised. If we ship it, there's a high probability of field failure."

"What's the probability?"

Kristina hated this question. "I don't have data on this specific contamination, but coating adhesion failures in field environments typically show up in 15–30% of compromised units over the first year."

"So 70–85% would be fine?"

"That's not how reliability works."

"Kristina, I need a solution. Can we do a waiver? Use-as-is disposition? These are going into non-critical housings, right?"

"They're avionics housings. Everything in an aircraft is critical."

"You know what I mean. Not flight-control critical. Not safety-of-flight. We've done waivers before."

She had. Too many times. And every waiver came back to haunt them—field failures, customer complaints, engineering investigations, retrofit campaigns. The cost of those waivers always exceeded the cost of doing it right the first time. Always.

But in the moment, when the customer was waiting and the penalties were adding up, management always chose the waiver.

"I need an hour," Kristina said. "Let me assess options."

"One hour. Then we need a decision."

She handed the phone back to Mark.

Tom was watching her. He knew what was coming. They'd had this conversation a dozen times over the past three years. Management pressure. Customer pressure. Schedule pressure. Cost pressure. Always pressure to just ship it.

"He wants a waiver," Tom said. Not a question.

"He wants a solution."

"A waiver is not a solution."

Kristina looked at the quarantined parts. At the idle production line. At Mark, stressed and checking his watch. At Tom, frustrated because he knew the right answer but couldn't make the decision.

She was tired.

Not physically tired—though she was. She'd been up since 5:30, and there'd been a similar crisis two weeks ago, and one a month before that.

She was tired of fighting the same fight. Tired of being the person who said "no" when everyone else wanted to say "yes." Tired of quality problems being everyone's emergency and nobody's priority.

Tired of signing waivers that turned into field failures that turned into customer complaints that turned into everyone asking, "Why didn't Quality catch this?"

She thought about the three field failures they'd had in the past six months. The connector issue that cost $180K to retrofit. The seal failure that delayed a program four months.

The coating adhesion problem—exactly like this one—that caused 47 units to fail in customer operations.

Each time, she'd raised concerns. Each time, she'd been overridden. Each time, the cost of fixing it in the field was 50–100 times what it would have cost to fix it right.

She made a decision.

Not about the waiver. About something bigger.

"Tom, call the customer. Tell them we have a quality hold and we need four days. No waiver. No use-as-is. We're going to rework it properly."

Tom looked surprised. "Management's going to push back."

"Let them. Call the customer."

While Tom made the call, Kristina walked back to her office. She pulled out a notebook and wrote at the top: "How much is poor quality actually costing us?"

She'd asked this question before, usually in moments like this. But she'd never actually answered it. The quality reports showed scrap and rework costs—about $3.2 million per year. That number got reported to management, who looked at it, said "We need to reduce scrap," and nothing changed.

But Kristina knew that $3.2 million was just the visible tip. Underneath was everything else—the premium freight, the customer credits, the engineering hours spent firefighting, the delayed launches, the lost contracts.

Nobody tracked that. Nobody added it up. Nobody saw the full picture.

She decided right then: She was going to find out the real number. All of it. And she was going to show management exactly what poor quality was costing them.

Then she was going to fix it. Not with more inspection. Not with more testing. Not with more firefighting.

With prevention.

She'd spent 20 years in quality—at defense contractors and small machine shops, in aerospace and medical devices. She'd seen prevention work when companies committed to it. And she'd seen quality death spirals when they didn't.

Aegis was in a death spiral. Firefighting consumed 80% of her team's time. They had no time for prevention. Which meant more fires. Which meant more firefighting. The cycle accelerated every year.

It had to stop.

She was going to make it stop.

Two Weeks Later: Mapping the Real Costs.

Kristina sat in the conference room with Tom and Sarah Chen, her other quality engineer, who handled supplier quality. On the whiteboard, she'd drawn four boxes:

PREVENTION | APPRAISAL | INTERNAL FAILURE
EXTERNAL FAILURE

"Here's what we're doing," Kristina said. "We're going to map every dollar Aegis spends dealing with poor quality. Not just what's in our department budget. Everything."

Sarah looked at the boxes. "What's the difference between these?"

"Cost of Poor Quality model," Kristina said. "Four categories. Prevention is money we spend to keep defects from happening—things like supplier audits, design validation, training. Appraisal is money we spend finding defects before they ship—inspection, testing, audits. Internal failure is defects we find before the customer sees them—scrap, rework, sorting. External failure is defects that reach the customer—warranty, returns, penalties, lost contracts."

Tom was already nodding. "And I bet we spend almost nothing on prevention and a fortune on external failure."

"That's what I want to prove. With real numbers."

Over the next two weeks, they dug through budgets, pulled reports, interviewed department heads, traced costs.

Week 1: Finding Prevention and Appraisal

Prevention was easy to find because there was so little of it. Kristina's quality budget showed:
- Supplier audits: $180K per year
- Design validation testing: $280K per year
- Training programs: $120K per year
- Process capability studies: $40K per year

Total prevention spending: **$620K**

Appraisal took longer because it was spread across departments.

Quality Department:
- Incoming inspection: $480K (2 inspectors full-time)
- In-process inspection: $920K (4 inspectors full-time)

- Final inspection and test: $680K (2 inspectors + equipment)

Manufacturing:
- First article inspection: $140K
- Process audits: $60K

Engineering:
- Design reviews: $180K (time spent)

Total appraisal spending: **$2.46M**

Week 2: The Hidden Costs

Internal failure started with the obvious—scrap and rework from the quality reports. But as they dug deeper, they found costs buried everywhere.

Quality Department tracked:
- Scrap material: $1.8M
- Rework labor: $1.4M

But that wasn't everything.

Manufacturing tracked "unplanned downtime." When Kristina and Tom analyzed it, they found quality issues caused 340 hours of line downtime in the past year.

Tom calculated: "340 hours at $150 per hour labor cost, but the real cost is lost production. Line 4 produces 12 units per hour. Margin per unit is about $1,800. So 340 hours means 4,080 lost units, which is $7.3 million in lost margin."

They found more:
- Material review board time: $240K (engineering + quality + manufacturing time spent dispositioning nonconforming material)
- Sorting and containment: $380K (when defects are found, someone has to sort good from bad)
- Re-inspection after rework: $290K
- Extra inventory held for quality issues: $420K (tied-up cash)

Total internal failure: **$12.1M**

Then came external failure. This was the big one.

Sarah pulled customer complaint data:
- Warranty claims paid: $1.8M

6

- Field service costs: $960K
- Customer returns processing: $180K

But Tom reminded them, "That's just direct costs. What about customer credits?"

They found them in the sales department budget:
- Customer credits and allowances: $2.4M
- Contractual penalties for late delivery: $1.1M

Kristina remembered the coating adhesion failure from six months ago. The customer had threatened to switch suppliers. Sales had negotiated an $800K credit to keep the contract. That wasn't labeled "quality cost" in any budget—it was "customer relationship management."

They kept digging.

Premium freight—rushing parts to customers because of quality delays: $890K (buried in logistics budget)

Tom interviewed the engineering director about engineering time spent on field failures instead of new product development. About 40% of engineering time went to firefighting quality issues. Engineering budget was $4.2M. That meant $1.68M of engineering time was reactive, not proactive.

Then the really big costs, the ones nobody tracked because they weren't direct expenses.

Lost contracts. Kristina pulled up three recent bids where Aegis had been competitive on price and performance but lost on quality reputation.

The surveillance pod follow-up: $11M over 4 years. The customer had told Sales: "Your technical solution is strong, but we've had too many quality issues. We can't risk it on this program." Lost to competitor.

Expected revenue loss: **$11M**

The radar housing program: delayed six months due to quality issues, causing customer to push out their deployment schedule. Customer billed Aegis $680K in penalty. But the real cost was the six-month delay on the follow-up order—an estimated $5M in deferred revenue.

And reputation costs. One customer had mandated 100% incoming inspection on all Aegis parts due to quality history. That meant every part Aegis shipped got inspected at the customer's facility, and the customer charged Aegis for that inspection time. $400 per lot. They shipped 120 lots per year. That was $48K per year in perpetuity until they proved their quality was reliable.

After two weeks, Kristina and Tom sat down with the complete picture.

The Quality P&L

Kristina formatted it like a profit and loss statement:

AEGIS AVIATION: COST OF POOR QUALITY
Annual Revenue: $120M | Employees: 400

PREVENTION COSTS

Supplier audits & development	$180K
Design validation & testing	$250K
Training programs	$110K
Process capability studies	$60K

TOTAL PREVENTION	$600K (2.0% of COPQ)

APPRAISAL COSTS

Incoming inspection	$380K
In-process inspection	$720K
Final inspection & test	$280K
First article inspection	$80K
Process audits	$40K

TOTAL APPRAISAL	$1.5M (5.0% of COPQ)

INTERNAL FAILURE COSTS

Scrap material	$1.4M
Rework labor	$1.1M
Line downtime (lost margin)	$3.2M
Material review board	$240K
Sorting & containment	$480K
Re-inspection after rework	$280K
Excess inventory (quality hold)	$200K

TOTAL INTERNAL FAILURE	$6.9M (23.0% of COPQ)

EXTERNAL FAILURE COSTS

Warranty & field service	$2.1M
Customer returns	$140K
Customer credits & allowances	$1.8M
Contractual penalties	$880K
Premium freight (quality delays)	$680K
Engineering time (firefighting)	$1.2M
Lost contracts (quality reputation)	$11M
Delayed revenue (schedule impact)	$3M
Increased customer inspection	$200K

TOTAL EXTERNAL FAILURE: $21M   (70.0%   of COPQ)

TOTAL COST OF POOR QUALITY $30M
AS % OF REVENUE: 25.0%

Kristina stared at the number. Twenty-five percent of revenue was being consumed by poor quality.

Tom looked stunned. "We're spending 35 times more on external failures than on prevention."

Sarah did the math differently. "If we spent just 10% of what we're losing to external failures on prevention instead, that's $2.1 million in prevention—we could probably cut external failures in half. That would be a $10 million swing."

Kristina knew the relationship wasn't quite that linear, but Sarah wasn't wrong. Every dollar spent on prevention saved ten to a hundred dollars downstream. The math was undeniable.

She scheduled a meeting with the VP of operations.

The Pitch

Kristina walked into the VP's office with a one-page summary and the backup data. "I need twenty minutes," she said.

The VP glanced at his calendar. "You've got fifteen. What's this about?"

On one page in front of him. She put one number at the top: "$30.0M"

"That's what poor quality cost us last year. Twenty-five percent of our revenue."

The VP looked at the number. Looked at her. "Our quality reports show $3.2 million."

"That's scrap and rework. That's what we track. This is everything, including costs buried in operations, engineering, sales, and logistics. Including lost contracts. Including delayed revenue."

She walked him through it. Prevention: $600K. Appraisal: $1.5M. Internal failure: $6.9M. External failure: $21M.

"The coating contamination two weeks ago? The one you wanted to waive? We reworked it properly. It cost us $160K and four days. But if we'd shipped it with a waiver, based on the adhesion failure we had six months ago, we'd be looking at 15–30% field failure rate. That's 36 to 72 units failing in customer operations. At $12,000 per field retrofit, that's $432K to $864K. Plus the customer relationship damage."

The VP was reading the breakdown. "These lost contract numbers, $22 million on the surveillance pod, that's speculative."

"It's documented. Sales told the customer we were competitive on price and performance. Customer said, 'We can't risk your quality on this program.' They gave it to our competitor. The bid was worth $22 million."

"We can't change the past."

"No. But we can change what happens next. We've got six active bids right now. If our quality reputation costs us one of those bids, we're looking at another $8 to $15 million in lost revenue."

The VP set down the paper. "What are you proposing?"

"A prevention fund. $500,000 to start. I want to invest it in the highest-leverage prevention opportunities, supplier capability improvements, design validation, process capability, the things that prevent defects from happening in the first place."

"You already have a quality budget."

"My budget is consumed by appraisal and firefighting. We spend 95% of our time finding and fixing problems, and 5% preventing them. That's backwards. Every study shows prevention is 10 to 100 times cheaper than fixing failures downstream."

"Show me."

Kristina pulled out a second sheet—the hydraulic seal supplier issue she and Tom had analyzed.

10

"We've had seal failures on three programs over the past two years. Root cause: supplier's oven temperature control is inadequate. Their process capability is $Cp = 1.1$, barely capable. They're producing 3% defective seals."

She walked him through the math:

Prevention option: Co-fund oven control upgrade with supplier

- Aegis investment: $50K (supplier matches)
- Timeline: 8 weeks
- Expected improvement: Defect rate from 3% to <0.5%

Cost of not preventing:

- Production rework: 240 failures over 2 years × $800 per failure = $192K
- Field failures: 40 units over 2 years × $12K per field retrofit = $480K
- Customer relationship impact: Quality issue already flagged on one program
- Expected total cost: $672K

"ROI: 13.4:1"

"And that's one supplier, one component," Kristina said. "I've identified twelve high-impact opportunities like this. Total prevention investment: $480K. Expected savings over two years: $6.4M."

The VP studied the numbers. "If I give you $500K, what's the guarantee that these savings happen?"

"I'll track every dollar. Monthly updates showing investment versus realized savings. If the ROI doesn't materialize in six months, we shut it down."

Silence. The VP was doing mental math—probability, risk, payback.

Finally: "You have approval for $500K. But I want quarterly reviews showing actual results, not projections. And if this is going to work, you need to change how we think about quality. Right now, quality is the department that slows things down and says no. That has to change."

"That's exactly what I'm trying to fix," Kristina said. "Quality shouldn't be the police. We should be the people who make it easier to do the right thing."

"Then prove it."

The Work Begins

Kristina walked back to her office with the approval. Tom and Sarah were waiting.

"We got it," she said. "Half a million. Six months to prove it works."

Tom grinned. "Where do we start?"

Kristina opened her notebook to the list of prevention opportunities they'd identified. "The seal supplier. Highest ROI, shortest payback. Sarah, you're going to lead that one. Visit their facility next week. Assess their capability. Build the development plan."

Sarah nodded. "I'll set it up."

"Tom, you're going to help me build business cases for the next tier—the connector qualification testing, the thermal validation, the coating process improvement. We need solid ROI calculations, so when we go back for the next round of funding, the numbers are bulletproof."

She looked at the quality P&L still on her desk. $30 million consumed by poor quality. $600K spent on prevention.

The ratio was insane. But it was about to change.

For the first time in three years, Kristina felt something other than frustration.

She felt hope.

Not because the problem was solved, it wasn't. They'd just scratched the surface.

But because they'd done something nobody at Aegis had done before: They'd made the full cost of poor quality visible. They'd quantified the pain. They'd shown leadership exactly what firefighting was costing them.

And they'd gotten approval to try a different approach.

Prevention wasn't glamorous. It didn't involve heroic firefighting or dramatic rescues. It was methodical, patient work—fixing root causes, building capability, designing quality in instead of inspecting it out.

But it was the only way to break the cycle.

Kristina picked up her phone and called Sarah. "When you visit the supplier next week, take pictures of their oven controls. I want to show people what $50K buys us versus what $672K costs us."

"Will do."

She hung up and looked at Tom. "Ready to do this?"

12

"Ready."
They got to work.

Chapter 2 — The Lever: Why a Dollar of Prevention Is Worth a Hundred Dollars of Cure

Kristina had $500K and six months to prove prevention worked. The easy part was getting the money. The hard part was choosing where to spend it. She sat in her office with Tom and Sarah, looking at the list they'd compiled during the COPQ analysis. Forty-two quality issues. Each one a potential prevention project. Each one with a different root cause, different cost, different ROI.

"We can't fix everything at once," Tom said. "We need a win. Something we can point to in three months and say 'Look, prevention works.'"

Sarah pulled up her notes. "The seal supplier has the best numbers. I pulled our CAPA database—we've had 23 corrective actions related to seal defects in the past 2 years. We're already paying for their defects—3% reject rate in production, field failures every few months. If we fix their process capability, we eliminate a chronic problem."

Kristina agreed. The seal supplier—Precision Seals, a 50-person shop based in Ohio—had been a quality headache for three years. Every program that used their elastomer seals had issues. The seals were inconsistent, some too brittle, some too rigid, just enough variation to cause problems.

The engineering solutions were always the same: tighten inspection, add testing, sort the bad ones. But that didn't fix the root cause. The supplier's process was incapable.

"Okay," Kristina said. "Sarah, this is your project. I want you to visit their facility, assess their capability, and come back with a development plan. Tom, you work with Sarah to build the business case—prevention cost versus failure cost. I want the numbers rock solid."

Sarah nodded. "When do I go?"

"Tomorrow. Spend two days on-site. Talk to their quality manager, watch the process, pull their data. Find out why their Cp/Cpk is only 1.1."

"What's my budget for the fix?" Sarah asked.

"That depends on the ROI," Kristina said. "If we can justify it, we'll co-fund with them. But I need to see the numbers first."

Week 1: The Supplier Visit

Sarah flew to Ohio the next morning. Precision Seals was located in an industrial park outside Dayton—a single-story building with a small office area and a 15,000-square-foot manufacturing floor.

Jim Morrison, the owner, met her at the door. "You must be Sarah. Come on in. I've got to say, I'm nervous about this visit. Are we in trouble?"

Sarah smiled. "Not at all. We're trying to prevent problems, not assign blame. I want to understand your process so we can help improve it."

Jim relaxed a little. "Well, let me show you around."

The facility was clean and organized. They molded elastomer seals for various customers—aerospace, medical, industrial. The process was straightforward: mix raw materials, mold under heat and pressure, cure in an oven, inspect.

Sarah watched the cure process—the step where quality problems originated. The oven was 15 years old, a batch-type unit with manual controls. An operator, Maria, set the temperature dial and timer, then monitored a strip chart recorder.

"How do you control cure temperature?" Sarah asked Maria.

"I set it to 350 degrees for 4 hours," Maria said. "But it's tricky. When I load a full batch, the temperature drops 15–20 degrees. I have to turn the dial up, wait for it to recover, then turn it back down. If I overshoot, the seals come out too hard. If I undershoot, they're too soft."

Sarah looked at the strip chart. The temperature trace looked like a rollercoaster—335°F to 368°F over the four-hour cure cycle.

"Do you have temperature sensors in multiple zones?" Sarah asked.

"Just one sensor," Maria said. "It's in the middle of the oven. The corners are probably different temperatures, but we don't measure them."

Sarah spent the afternoon with Tom Chen, Precision Seals' quality manager (not related to Kristina's Tom), reviewing their data. Over the past year:

- 3.2% of seals failed internal leak testing
- 0.8% failed dimensional checks (hardness out of spec)
- Total internal reject rate: 4.0%

Tom Chen pulled up their process capability study. "We ran Cp/Cpk analysis last year. Cure temperature specification is 350°F ±10°F. Our Cp is 1.1, Cpk is 0.95. Barely capable."

Sarah did the math in her head. Cp of 1.1 meant the process variation was almost as wide as the specification. Cpk of 0.95 meant the process was off-center—not centered on the target temperature.

"What's causing the off-center?" Sarah asked.

"The oven runs hot," Tom said. "Average temperature is about 353°F instead of 350°F. The operator, Maria, tries to compensate, but it drifts."

Sarah had seen enough. She'd use a simple *"5 Whys analysis"* when she got back to document the root cause:

1. Why are seals inconsistent? → Because cure temperature varies
2. Why does temperature vary? → Because operator must adjust manually
3. Why manual adjustment? → Because oven has no automatic control
4. Why no automatic control? → Because oven is 15 years old with basic controls
5. Why no upgrade? → Because capital wasn't prioritized

The root cause was clear: inadequate temperature control. Manual control couldn't maintain the stability needed for a 20-degree temperature window. The operator was doing her best, but the equipment wasn't capable.

Week 2: Building the Business Case

Back at Aegis, Sarah sat down with Tom Rodriguez to build the business case. This was the heart of the corrective action—not just fixing the immediate problem but preventing it from recurring. They'd use elements of 8D problem-solving: define the problem, identify root cause, develop permanent corrective actions, and verify effectiveness.

"Here's what I found," Sarah said. "Their oven has manual temperature control—literally a dial and a strip chart. One sensor. No feedback control. The operator has to adjust manually when temperature drifts."

Tom pulled up a whiteboard. "Let's map the failure cost first. Then we'll figure out what it costs to fix."

Current State: Cost of Supplier Defects

They started with production detection costs—defects found at Aegis during incoming inspection and production.

16

Tom pulled the data:
- Seals received from Precision: 8,000 per year (across 3 programs)
- Defect rate at Aegis: 3% (240 seals rejected per year)

Cost per production defect:
- Reject the seal: $80 (material cost)
- Expedited order replacements: $120 (premium shipping)
- Line delay while waiting: 4 hours × $150/hour = $600
- Inspection of replacement: $40
- Total per production defect: **$840**

Production cost: 240 defects × $840 = **$201,600 per year**

However, that wasn't the full cost. Some defects escaped to the field.

Tom pulled field failure data:
- Field escape rate: 0.5% (about 40 seals per year reached customer and failed)

Cost per field failure:
- Expedited replacement seal: $400 (overnight shipping + priority handling)
- Field service labor: $2,400 (technician travel + installation)
- Customer aircraft downtime: $8,000 (estimated based on customer complaints)
- Customer relationship impact: $1,200 (credits and goodwill gestures)
- Total per field failure: **$12,000**

Field failure cost: 40 failures × $12,000 = **$480,000 per year**

Then there were the indirect costs. After the third field failure on one program, the customer had mandated an incoming inspection of all Aegis seals instead of sampling. That meant every seal got inspected twice—once at Precision Seals (their internal QC) and once at Aegis (incoming inspection).

Additional inspection cost: $0.50 per seal × 8,000 seals = $4,000 per year (and growing as volumes increased)

Total annual cost of seal defects: **$685,600**

Over a typical 3-year program life: **$2,056,800**

Tom wrote the number on the whiteboard. Sarah stared at it.

"Two million dollars," Sarah said. "For one component, from one supplier."

"Now let's figure out what it costs to fix," Tom said.

The Prevention Option

Sarah had talked to Jim Morrison at Precision Seals about upgrading their oven controls. She'd also consulted with a process controls vendor who specialized in thermal systems.

The fix required three things:

1. Automated Temperature Control System
   - Replace manual dial with PLC (programmable logic controller)
   - Install three temperature sensors (instead of one) to monitor all zones
   - Implement closed-loop feedback control (PLC automatically adjusts heating elements to maintain setpoint)
   - Cost: $75,000 (equipment + installation)

2. Data Logging and SPC
   - Install data acquisition system to log temperature every 10 seconds
   - Implement statistical process control (SPC) software
   - Train operators on control charts and response procedures
   - Cost: $15,000 (software + training)

3. Process Validation
   - Run capability studies after upgrade
   - Validate seal properties across operating range
   - Update process specifications
   - Cost: $10,000 (Aegis engineering time + testing)

Total prevention investment: **$100,000**

The bigger issue was that Precision Seals couldn't afford $100K. Jim Morrison had been honest: "We're a small shop. We don't have $100K sitting around. Our profit margin on your seals is about 15%. That's $96K per year. You're asking me to invest more than a year's profit."

Sarah understood. Smaller suppliers lived on thin margins. They couldn't self-fund major capital improvements, even when those improvements would benefit everyone.

She proposed cost-sharing:

- Aegis funds: $50,000 (50% of capital equipment + validation)
- Precision Seals funds: $50,000 (50% of capital equipment + ongoing maintenance)
- Repayment structure: Aegis recoups investment through negotiated piece-part price adjustment over 3 years ($16,667 per year)

Value proposition for Precision Seals:

- Reduce internal reject rate from 4% to <0.5% (saves $80K per year in scrap)
- Increase capacity by 4% (frees-up capacity from reduced scrap = $60K per year in potential new business)
- Improve quality reputation with all customers (not just Aegis)
- Net payback for their $50K investment: <1 year

Jim Morrison agreed to the deal.

The ROI Calculation

Tom built the complete lifecycle cost comparison:

SCENARIO A: No Prevention (Continue Current State)

Annual costs:

- Production defects: $201,600
- Field failures: $480,000
- Extra inspection: $4,000
- Total annual cost: $685,600

3-year program cost: **$2,056,800**

SCENARIO B: Prevention Investment

Upfront costs:

- Aegis investment: $50,000
- Precision Seals investment: $50,000 (not Aegis' cost, but shown for completeness)

- Total investment: $100,000

Expected improvement:
- New process capability target: $Cp \geq 1.67$, $Cpk \geq 1.50$
- Expected defect rate: <0.5% (down from 3%)
- Expected field escape rate: <0.05% (down from 0.5%)

Annual costs after prevention:
- Production defects: 40 defects × $840 = $33,600 (83% reduction)
- Field failures: 4 failures × $12,000 = $48,000 (90% reduction)
- Extra inspection: $4,000 (continues until demonstrated reliability)

Total annual cost: **$85,600**

3-year program cost: $50,000 investment + $85,600 × 3 years = **$306,800**

Net savings over 3 years: $2,056,800 $306,800 = **$1,750,000**

Return on investment: $1,750,000 ÷ $50,000 = 35:1

Payback period: $50,000 ÷ $600,000 annual savings = 1 month

Tom looked at the numbers. "These are almost too good. Let me run a sensitivity analysis."

He tested pessimistic assumptions:
- What if prevention only reduces defects by 50% (not 83%)? → ROI still 12:1
- What if investment is 50% higher ($75K)? → ROI still 23:1
- What if we only get 2 years of benefit (program ends early)? → ROI still 24:1

Even in worst-case scenarios, the ROI was compelling.

"Bulletproof," Tom said. "Let's show Kristina."

Week 3: Leadership Approval

Kristina reviewed the business case with Tom and Sarah. The numbers were solid. The plan was clear. The supplier was committed.

She scheduled a meeting with the VP of operations.

"I've got our first prevention project ready," Kristina said. "I need your approval for $50K."

She walked him through it:

- The problem: 3% defect rate from seal supplier, costing $685K per year
- The root cause: inadequate oven temperature control
- The solution: automated controls + SPC
- The investment: $50K (co-funded with supplier)
- The expected ROI: 35:1
- The payback: 1 month

The VP studied the numbers. "What's the risk if this doesn't work?"

"Low," Kristina said. "The root cause is clear—manual temperature control can't maintain stability. Automated controls are proven technology. The process controls vendor guarantees the capability improvement."

"And if Precision Seals goes out of business?"

"We've verified their financials. They're stable. And if they did fail, we own the equipment—it's installed at their facility, but contractually it's ours. We could move it to a new supplier."

"What about other suppliers? Are we going to do this with everyone?"

"Only where it makes sense," Kristina said. "We've categorized suppliers into strategic, capable, and problematic. Precision Seals is a strategic—critical component, single source. We'll invest in strategic suppliers. For capable suppliers, we'll maintain and monitor. For problematic suppliers, we'll either develop them or replace them."

The VP approved the $50K.

"One more thing," Kristina added. "I want you to visit Precision Seals with me next month. See the old oven versus the new controls. I want leadership to understand what $50K buys us versus what $2M costs us."

"I'll make time," the VP said.

Weeks 4–12: Implementation

The oven control upgrade took eight weeks to complete.

Week 4: Equipment ordered. Long lead-time item was the PLC system (4 weeks delivery).

Weeks 5–7: While waiting for equipment, Tom Chen at Precision Seals prepared the installation plan. They'd need to shut down the oven for three days during installation.

Week 8: Equipment arrived. Installation crew began work.

Sarah made a visit during the installation. The new system was impressive:

- Three temperature sensors (front, middle, back of oven)
- PLC cabinet with touchscreen interface
- Automated control valves on heating elements
- Data-logging system capturing temperature every 10 seconds

Maria, the operator, watched nervously. "Is this going to be complicated?"

The installer showed her the touchscreen. "You'll load the parts, press START, and the system handles everything. The screen shows you real-time temperature in all three zones. If something goes wrong, it alerts you."

Weeks 9–10: System commissioned and debugged. Initial test runs looked promising. Temperature stability was within ±2°F (versus ±18°F before).

Week 11: Process capability study. Sarah and Tom Rodriguez visited to observe.

They ran 30 consecutive batches—300 seals—measuring cure temperature and seal properties.

Results:

- Cure temperature: 350°F ±2.5°F consistently
- Process capability: Cp = 2.1, Cpk = 2.0 (more than adequate)
- Seal hardness: 99.7% within specification
- Leak test pass rate: 99.4% (reject rate 0.6%, down from 3.2%)

Sarah was thrilled. "Cp of 2.1 means this process is highly capable. We've gone from barely capable to excellent."

Tom Chen was relieved. "Best of all, Maria loves the new sensors and software. She said it's so much easier—she just loads the oven, and the system does the rest."

Week 12: First production shipment of seals from the improved process arrived at Aegis.

Tom Rodriguez ran incoming inspection. Out of 200 seals: 199 passed, 1 rejected for a minor cosmetic issue (not a functional defect).

Defect rate: 0.5%

The improvement was real.

Month 4: Tracking Results

Kristina implemented a tracking system to measure actual savings versus projected. This was critical for CAPA effectiveness verification—proving that corrective actions actually worked, not just assuming they did.

Projected 3-year savings (from business case):
- Reduced production defects: $503,400
- Reduced field failures: $1,296,000
- Total: $1,799,400

Actual results (first 3 months after implementation):
Month 1:
- Seals received: 600
- Defects found: 4 (0.67%)
- Expected defects at old rate: 18
- Avoided defects: 14
- Savings: 14 × $840 = $11,760
- Field failures: 0 (vs. 1 expected)
- Field failure savings: 1 × $12,000 = $12,000
- Month 1 total savings: $23,760

Month 2:
- Seals received: 650
- Defects found: 3 (0.46%)
- Avoided defects: 17
- Savings: 17 × $840 = $14,280
- Field failures: 0 (vs. 1 expected)
- Field failure savings: $12,000
- Month 2 total savings: $26,280

Month 3:
- Seals received: 700
- Defects found: 5 (0.71%)
- Avoided defects: 16
- Savings: 16 × $840 = $13,440
- Field failures: 0 (vs. 2 expected)
- Field failure savings: 2 × $12,000 = $24,000
- Month 3 total savings: $37,440

Three-month realized savings: **$87,480**

Annualized savings rate: $87,480 × 4 = **$349,920**

The ROI was tracking even better than projected. At this rate, payback would be 6 weeks, not 1 month (still excellent).

Month 5: The VP's Visit

Kristina and the VP of operations flew to Ohio to visit Precision Seals.

Jim Morrison gave them a tour. He showed them the old oven controls—the manual dial and strip chart recorder—sitting on a shelf now.

"That's what we used for 15 years," Jim said. "Maria did her best, but you can't hit ±5 degrees with a manual dial."

Then he showed them the new system—the PLC cabinet, touchscreen, and three temperature sensors.

"This is what $100K buys," Jim said. "Look at this." He pulled up the temperature chart on the screen. Three lines—front, middle, back zones—all within 2 degrees of setpoint. Flat lines, not rollercoasters.

The VP studied the chart. "What's this done for your business?"

"Our reject rate is down from 4% to 0.5%," Jim said. "That's $80K per year in scrap we're not generating. Plus, we've freed up capacity—we can take on new customers without adding a second oven. And our customers are noticing. We've gotten compliments from three customers in the past two months about improved quality."

He looked at Kristina. "This investment didn't just help Aegis. It helped us become a better company."

On the flight back, the VP was quiet for a while. Then he said, "I get it now. Prevention isn't about spending money. *It's about investing in capability.* And the math isn't even close—$50K to prevent $2M in failures."

"Exactly," Kristina said.

"How many more opportunities like this do we have?"

Kristina pulled out her list. "Eleven more in the high-ROI category. Total investment: $430K. Expected 3-year savings: $5.8M."

"Let's do them," the VP said. "All of them."

Month 6: Quarterly Review

Kristina presented the first quarterly update to leadership. She brought data:

Project: Seal Supplier Capability Improvement
Investment:
- Aegis: $50,000
- Precision Seals: $50,000 (co-funded)
- Total: $100,000

Timeline:
- Week 1: Supplier assessment
- Weeks 4–8: Equipment procurement and installation
- Weeks 9–11: Validation
- Week 12: First production delivery
- Months 4–6: Results tracking

Results (6 months):
- Defect rate: 3.0% → 0.6% (80% reduction)
- Production rework cost avoided: $88,200
- Field failures avoided: 6 units (expected vs. actual)
- Field failure cost avoided: $72,000
- Total realized savings: $160,200
- ROI to date: 3.2:1 (at 6 months)
- Projected 3-year ROI: 35:1

Process improvements:
- Supplier process capability: Cp 1.1 → 2.1
- Oven temperature stability: ±18°F → ±2°F
- Supplier internal reject rate: 4.0% → 0.5%

Supplier relationship:
- Precision Seals' capacity increased 4%
- Quality reputation improved with other customers
- Supplier actively proposing improvements on other components

The CEO, who'd been silent, spoke up. "This is one supplier, one component. What's the bigger picture?"

Kristina pulled up the next slide. "We've identified 42 chronic quality issues. We've categorized them by ROI. The top 12 have ROI over 20:1. We've completed one. We're ready to start three more."

She showed the pipeline:

- Connector qualification testing: $45K investment, projected $1.2M savings, 27:1 ROI
- Coating process automation: $80K investment, projected $1.8M savings, 23:1 ROI
- Thermal validation protocol: $35K investment, projected $840K savings, 24:1 ROI

"My request," Kristina said, "is approval to proceed with these three projects. Total investment: $160K from the remaining prevention fund. Expected savings over 3 years: $3.8M."

The CEO looked at the VP of operations. "Your call."

"Approved," the VP said. "And Kristina, I want you to present this seal supplier case study at the next all-hands meeting. Everyone needs to see what prevention looks like."

The Shift Begins

Two weeks later, Kristina stood in front of 200 employees at the quarterly all-hands meeting.

She showed pictures of the old oven controls versus the new system. She showed the temperature charts—rollercoaster versus flat lines. She showed the cost data—$2M in failure costs versus $50K in prevention investment.

"This is what prevention looks like," Kristina said. "It's not more inspections. It's not more tests. It's fixing root causes. It's building capability. It's investing in systems that make quality automatic." She paused.

"For the past three years, we've been firefighting. Eighty percent of our time finding and fixing problems. Twenty percent preventing them. That ratio is about to flip. We're going to spend most of our time preventing problems. And when problems do occur, we're going to learn from them so they never happen again."

After the meeting, an engineer approached her. "That seal supplier project—can we do something similar with the connector supplier? We've had three field failures this year."

"That's exactly what we're doing next," Kristina said. "Come by my office tomorrow. Let's talk."

A manufacturing supervisor stopped her in the hallway. "I've got an idea for a poka-yoke fixture that would prevent the assembly errors we keep seeing on Line 3. Can I get funding for that?"

"Bring me the business case," Kristina said. "Show me prevention cost versus failure cost. If the ROI makes sense, we'll fund it."

That evening, Kristina sat in her office reviewing the past six months.

Six months ago, she'd been exhausted. Firefighting. Signing waivers. Being blamed for problems she didn't cause.

Now, she had a prevention fund. She had leadership support. She had projects in the pipeline. She had engineers and supervisors asking for prevention funding.

The culture was starting to shift.

People were starting to see quality differently—not as inspection and testing, but as capability and prevention.

The seal supplier project had proven the concept. $50K invested. $160K saved in six months. On track for $1.75M over three years.

But more important than the savings, it had shown everyone what prevention looked like in practice. Not theory. Not consultants. Just methodical root-cause analysis, capability improvement, and measurement.

Tom knocked on Kristina's door. "Sarah just sent the connector supplier assessment. They've got similar issues—inadequate process controls. She's building the business case now."

"Good," Kristina said. "Let's keep moving."

The transformation was just beginning. They'd fixed one supplier, one component. They had forty-one more opportunities to pursue.

The hardest part was behind them—proving that prevention worked. Now it was about scaling it.

Building prevention into how Aegis designed products, selected suppliers, ran processes, and made decisions.

That work started in the next phase.

Chapter 3 — The Architect: Why Quality Can't Be Delegated

Nine months into the prevention transformation, Kristina faced a problem she hadn't anticipated.

The seal supplier project had worked. The connector qualification was working. The coating automation was working. Prevention fund projects were delivering 25:1 average ROI.

But Kristina was exhausted again.

Not from firefighting, those calls had dropped by 60%. She was exhausted from fighting a different battle: getting people to choose prevention.

Every design review, she had to push engineers to complete DFMEA. Every supplier selection, she had to argue with purchasing about capability assessment. Every production ramp, she had to convince operations to run capability studies first.

The prevention projects proved the math. But they didn't change how decisions got made.

She was still the bottleneck. If she wasn't in the room, prevention got skipped.

The Pattern

Kristina sat in her office reviewing the past week's decisions:

Monday: Engineering released a design for a new gimbal housing without completing DFMEA. She found out two days later when manufacturing flagged producibility issues. Now they were redesigning components that were already in tooling.

Tuesday: Purchasing selected a new machining supplier based on lowest bid—$18 per part versus $22 from the incumbent. Nobody assessed the supplier's process capability. First article inspection showed 40% of parts out of tolerance. Now they were scrambling to find an alternate supplier.

Wednesday: Operations ramped Line 5 to full production without running capability studies. By Friday, first pass yield was 76%. They were reworking 24% of output—exactly what capability studies would have predicted and prevented.

Thursday: A Program Manager approved an engineering change to reduce material cost by $3 per unit without calculating lifecycle cost impact. The change introduced a new failure mode that would cost $15K per field failure. Expected failures over program life: 20 units. That $3 saving just created $300K in future cost.

Each decision had seemed rational in the moment. Engineering was under schedule pressure. Purchasing was hitting cost targets. Operations was meeting output quotas. The Program Manager was improving margins.

However, every decision created quality problems that Kristina's team would spend the next six months fixing.

Tom knocked on her door. "You okay?"

"No, I'm really frustrated," Kristina said. "We've proven prevention works. But I still have to fight for it every single day. If I'm not in the meeting, prevention doesn't happen."

"We need to change the system," Tom said. "Right now, prevention is optional. People can skip DFMEA, skip capability assessment, skip process validation—and there's no consequence until something fails. By then, it's too late and too expensive."

Kristina knew he was right. Prevention projects addressed specific technical problems. But they didn't address the organizational problem: quality decisions were made without quality input.

She needed to change how decisions got made. Not through more meetings or more oversight. Through simple rules that made prevention the default choice.

Mapping Decision Points

Kristina gathered Tom and Sarah in the conference room. "We need to map where quality decisions happen and who makes them."

She drew a table on the whiteboard:

Decision point	Who decides now	Quality involved?	What goes wrong
Design release	Engineering manager	No (notified after)	Designs released with unresolved DFMEA items
Supplier selection	Purchasing	No (informed after selection)	Suppliers selected without capability assessment

Production ramp	Operations manager	No (asked to inspect more)	Processes ramped before capability proved
Engineering changes	Engineering manager	Sometimes (if they remember)	Changes create new failure modes
Waiver decisions	Program manager	Yes (but advisory only)	Waives signed under schedule pressure

Tom looked at the list. "Quality has zero decision authority. We can advise, but anyone can ignore us. Then when things fail, everyone asks 'Why didn't quality catch it?'"

"Exactly," Kristina said. "We need quality involved in decisions before they're made, not after. And we need clear rules about what's required."

The Simple Rules

Kristina spent the next week drafting simple decision rules. Not formal gate processes with escalation matrices and sign-off authority. Just clear expectations about what had to happen before certain decisions could be made.

RULE 1: No Design Released Without DFMEA

Before any design could be released to tooling or production:
- DFMEA must be completed by cross-functional team (Engineering, Manufacturing, Quality, Test)
- High-severity failure modes (Severity ≥ 8) must have prevention or detection plans documented
- Quality engineer must review and confirm DFMEA is complete

If engineering wanted to release a design without completing DFMEA, they had to escalate to VP of operations and explain why schedule was more important than preventing field failures.

RULE 2: No New Supplier Without Capability Assessment

Before any new supplier could be added to the approved supplier list:

- Supplier quality engineer must conduct on-site assessment
- Process capability data (Cp/Cpk) must be documented for critical characteristics
- Sample parts must pass first article inspection

If purchasing wanted to select a supplier without capability assessment, they had to escalate to VP of operations with lifecycle cost justification.

RULE 3: No Production Ramp Without Capability Proof

Before any process could ramp from pilot to full production:

- Process capability study must show Cp ≥1.33 for critical parameters
- First article inspection must pass
- 30-unit pilot run must achieve ≥95% First Pass Yield

If operations wanted to ramp without proving capability, they had to escalate to VP of operations and accept accountability for expected rework costs.

RULE 4: Engineering Changes Require Lifecycle Cost Analysis

Before any engineering change affecting cost, materials, or processes could be approved:

- Lifecycle cost analysis must compare total program cost (not just piece-part cost)
- Changes that increase expected COPQ must be approved by quality manager
- DFMEA must be updated to reflect new failure modes

RULE 5: Waivers Require Risk Assessment

Before any nonconformance could be dispositioned as "use-as-is":

- Root-cause analysis must be documented
- Field failure risk must be assessed (probability × consequence)
- Customer notification plan must be approved by quality manager

These weren't bureaucratic processes. They were simple checkpoints: "Before you do X, have you done Y?"

The key insight: make prevention the path of least resistance. Following the rules was easier than escalating exceptions.

The Pitch to Leadership

Kristina presented the five rules to the VP of operations.

"I need your backing on this," she said. "These rules only work if people know you'll support them."

The VP read through the list. "These seem reasonable. But I'm going to get pushback. Engineering will say it slows them down. Purchasing will say it limits their options. Operations will say it delays production ramps."

"Let me show you what not having these rules cost us last week," Kristina said.

She pulled up the four examples from Monday through Thursday:

"Design released without DFMEA": Now redesigning in tooling. Cost: $45K in scrap tooling + 3-week delay

"Supplier selected without assessment": 40% defect rate, scrambling for alternate supplier. Cost: $28K in rejected parts + 2-week delay + customer delivery risk

"Production ramped without capability proof": 76% first pass yield, reworking 24% of output. Cost: $1,200 per day in rework labor + schedule impact

"Engineering change without lifecycle cost": Created $300K in future field failure costs to save $3 per unit

Total cost of skipping prevention last week: **$373K** (not counting the future field failures)

"These five rules would have prevented all of this," Kristina said. "The time to complete DFMEA, assess a supplier, or run a capability study is measured in days or weeks. The cost of skipping them is measured in tens or hundreds of thousands of dollars."

The VP was quiet for a moment. Then: "You're right. But here's my concern—if we make these rules mandatory, we need to make sure quality can actually support them. Can you do supplier assessments within purchasing's timeline? Can you review DFMEAs without delaying design releases?"

"Yes," Kristina said. "If we know about decisions before they're made, instead of finding out after. Right now, we're reactive. These rules make us part of the decision process."

"Okay. I'll announce these rules at the next staff meeting. But Kristina—you need to make sure your team can execute. If these rules slow us down without improving quality, we'll revisit them."

"Fair," Kristina said.

Week 1: Announcing the Rules

At the next staff meeting, the VP of operations announced the five decision rules.

"Effective immediately, these are the expectations," he said. "No design released without DFMEA. No supplier selected without a capability assessment. No production ramp without capability proof. Any engineering changes require lifecycle cost analysis. Waivers require risk assessment."

He paused. "These aren't suggestions. These are requirements. If you want to make an exception, you escalate to me and explain why schedule or cost is more important than preventing failure. But I'm telling you right now—I'm going to ask, 'What's the expected cost of this failure?' and 'Why can't we prevent it?' So come prepared."

The engineering manager raised his hand. "What if DFMEA would delay a critical design release?"

"Then you come to me with the DFMEA status, the remaining risks, and your mitigation plan. And we decide together if the schedule risk outweighs the technical risk. But you don't skip DFMEA and hope nothing goes wrong."

The purchasing manager spoke up. "What if the supplier with best capability is 20% more expensive?"

"Then you show me the lifecycle cost comparison," the VP said. "If the capable supplier costs $22 per part but the incapable supplier will generate $8,000 in rework and field failures, the $22 supplier is cheaper. But you need to show me the math."

The operations manager asked, "What if the capability study shows Cp of 1.25 instead of 1.33? Do we stop the whole production ramp?"

"No," the VP said. "You come to me with the data and your plan. Maybe we ramp at 50% while we improve capability. Maybe we add temporary inspection. But we don't ramp to full production knowing we'll have 25% defects."

The message was clear: prevention was non-negotiable. Exceptions required escalation and justification.

Weeks 2–4: The Rules in Practice

The first few weeks were rocky. People tested the boundaries.

Design Release Test:

An engineering manager tried to release a design with DFMEA "90% complete—we'll finish the last 10% next week."

Tom reviewed the DFMEA. The "last 10%" included three high-severity failure modes without prevention plans.

Tom called the engineering manager. "I can't sign off on this. You've got three Severity 9 failure modes without prevention plans. Those need to be addressed before release."

"We're already behind schedule," the engineer said. "We'll address them during prototyping."

"That's exactly what we're trying to prevent," Tom said. "Addressing them now costs two weeks of design time. Addressing them in prototyping costs six weeks and $40K in prototype rework. Your call, do you want to escalate to the VP?"

The engineer paused. "No. We'll finish the DFMEA."

Two weeks later, the DFMEA flagged a thermal management issue that would have required redesign in prototyping. The team added cooling fins in the design phase. Cost: one week of design time. Savings: six weeks and $40K.

Supplier Selection Test:

Purchasing found a fastener supplier offering 30% cost savings. Sarah was asked to assess capability.

Sarah called the supplier. "Can you send me process capability data for the threading operation?"

"We don't track Cp/Cpk," the supplier said. "But we've been making fasteners for 20 years. We know what we're doing."

Sarah scheduled a site visit. The threading process used manual machines with no SPC. The operator relied on "feel" to know when to adjust.

Sarah pulled sample parts and measured them. Thread pitch variation was barely within spec. Estimated Cp: 0.9 (not capable).

She reported to purchasing: "This supplier will generate 8–10% defects. At our volume, that's 800–1,000 defective fasteners per year. Rework cost: $12 per fastener. Expected annual cost: $9,600–$12,000. The 30% price savings is $4,800 per year. Net: we lose $4,800–$7,200 per year."

Purchasing stayed with the incumbent supplier.

Production Ramp Test:

Operations wanted to ramp Line 3 to full production. Quality ran the capability study.

34

Results: Cp = 1.28 for a critical dimension (below the 1.33 requirement).

The operations supervisor argued: "1.28 is close enough. We'll watch it closely."

Tom showed him the data: "Cp of 1.28 predicts 2.3% defect rate. At full production, that's 160 defective units per month. Rework cost: $840 per unit. That's $134,400 per month."

"What do we need to do to get to 1.33?" the supervisor asked.

"The fixture is wearing. Replace it. Cost: $8,000. Timeline: one week."

The supervisor replaced the fixture. New Cp: 1.51. They ramped to full production with <0.5% defects.

Month 3: Changing Metrics

The rules were working, but Kristina knew they wouldn't stick without changing what people were measured on. She met with the VP of operations. "The rules are preventing bad decisions. But people are still optimizing for the wrong things. Engineers are measured on schedule, not quality. Purchasing is measured on cost savings, not total cost. Operations is measured on output, not first pass yield."

"What do you propose?" the VP asked.

"Change the metrics. Not drastically—just add quality to the equation."

She showed him the proposal:

Engineering Performance:
-   Current: 100% weight on schedule and features
-   Proposed: 70% schedule and features, 30% design quality (DFMEA completion, first pass prototype success, field failure rate)

Purchasing Performance:
-   Current: 100% weight on cost savings
-   Proposed: 60% cost savings, 40% supplier quality (defect rates, capability, delivery performance)

Operations Performance:
-   Current: 100% weight on output volume
-   Proposed: 60% output volume, 40% quality metrics (first pass yield, scrap rate, rework hours)

Program Management Performance:

- Current: 80% schedule, 20% cost
- Proposed: 50% schedule, 30% cost, 20% quality (customer satisfaction, field failures, warranty costs)

"This makes people accountable for quality outcomes, not just short-term outputs," Kristina said.

The VP approved it. "Phase it in over two quarters. Give people time to adjust."

Month 6: The Culture Shifts

Six months after implementing the decision rules, Kristina noticed that the culture starting to change.

"Engineers were completing DFMEA proactively." A design engineer approached Tom: "I'm starting DFMEA on the new sensor housing. Can you join the kickoff meeting next week?"

"You're starting DFMEA before I asked?" Tom said, surprised.

"Well, yeah," the engineer said. "I can't release the design without it. And last time we did DFMEA early, we caught three issues that would have been expensive to fix later. It's just part of the design process now."

"Purchasing was requesting capability data." A buyer called Sarah: "I've got three quotes for the machined bracket. Can you help me evaluate supplier capability? I don't want to pick the cheapest one and create a quality problem."

Sarah was stunned. Six months ago, Purchasing fought every capability assessment. Now they were asking for help.

"Operations was running capability studies before ramping." A supervisor scheduled a capability study for Line 4 without being told. "I'm not ramping until I know we can hit first pass yield targets," he said. "I don't want to spend three months reworking parts."

"Program Managers were asking about lifecycle costs." A Program Manager called Kristina: "Engineering proposed a design change to save $2 per unit. Before I approve it, can you help me understand if it creates any quality risks?"

Kristina was shocked. This was the same Program Manager who, six months ago, approved changes without thinking about quality impact.

"What changed?" Kristina asked.

"My performance review," the Program Manager admitted. "Twenty percent of my rating is quality metrics now. I can't afford field failures."

It wasn't perfect. People were still learning. There were still debates about capability requirements, risk assessments, and cost trade-offs.

But the fundamental shift had happened: Prevention was becoming the default, not the exception.

Month 9: The Test

Nine months after implementing the decision rules, the system faced its biggest test.

A critical program was behind schedule. The customer was threatening penalties. The Program Manager came to Kristina with a request: "We need to waive the capability requirement on Line 2. Current Cp is 1.15. I know the rule says 1.33, but we don't have time to improve the process. Can we get a waiver?"

Kristina looked at the data. "What's the predicted defect rate at Cp 1.15?"

"About 4%," the Program Manager admitted.

"And your production volume for the next six months?"

"2,000 units."

Kristina did the math. "Four percent of 2,000 units is 80 defects. Rework cost is $920 per unit. That's $73,600 in rework costs."

"I know," the Program Manager said. "But the penalty for late delivery is $120,000. If we don't ramp now, we'll miss the delivery date."

"What would it take to improve Cp from 1.15 to 1.33?"

The Program Manager pulled up the analysis. "Manufacturing engineering says we need to replace two worn fixtures and add temperature control to the bonding process. Cost: $18,000. Timeline: 10 days."

Kristina pulled up the calculator. "Okay, let's compare scenarios."

Scenario A: Ramp now with Cp 1.15
- Rework cost: $73,600
- Avoid late penalty: $0
- Total cost: $73,600

Scenario B: Delay 10 days, improve Cp to 1.33
- Process improvement: $18,000
- Rework cost (reduced): $9,200 (1% defect rate)
- Late penalty: $120,000
- Total cost: $147,200

Scenario C: Start ramping now + improve process in parallel
- Ramp at 50% rate while improving process (5-day delay)
- Meet most of delivery schedule
- Estimated penalty: $40,000 (partial late delivery)
- Process improvement: $18,000
- Rework cost (blend of rates): $28,000
- Total cost: $86,000

"Scenario C is best," Kristina said. "Start ramping at half rate while Manufacturing fixes the process. You'll deliver most parts on time, minimize the penalty, and reduce total rework. And you don't violate the capability rule—you're improving the process while managing schedule risk."

The Program Manager thought about it. "That could work. Let me talk to operations."

Operations agreed to the plan. They ramped at 50% while manufacturing replaced fixtures and added temperature control. Within a week, Cp improved to 1.42. They ramped to full rate.

Final results:
- Penalty paid: $35,000 (less than projected)
- Process improvement: $18,000
- Rework costs: $22,000 (mix of high and low defect rates)
- Total cost: $75,000

Still not great—but better than $147K (full delay) and better than the $73,600 that would have turned into $150K+ when field failures occurred.

More importantly: the Program Manager didn't ask for a waiver. He asked for help solving the problem within the constraints.

The New Normal

A year after implementing the prevention transformation, Kristina sat in her office reviewing progress.

COPQ Results:
- Starting point: $30M (25% of revenue)
- Current: $24M (20% of revenue)
- Improvement: $6M (20% reduction)

Quality Metrics:
- First pass yield: 84% → 89%
- Field failure rate: 0.8% → 0.5%

- Customer complaints: Down 42%
- Supplier defect rate: Down 38%

Prevention Metrics:
- Prevention spending: $600K → $1.8M (3× increase)
- Prevention ROI: 28:1 average across 12 projects
- DFMEA completion rate: 40% → 85%
- Supplier capability assessments: 15% → 75% (of new suppliers)

Cultural Indicators:
- Engineers completing DFMEA before being asked (85% of the time, up from 40%)
- Purchasing requesting capability assessments (most of the time, not all)
- Operations running capability studies proactively (more often than before)
- Program Managers asking about lifecycle costs (starting to happen)

But the most important indicator: Kristina wasn't fighting battles anymore.

The decision rules had made prevention automatic. Engineers didn't skip DFMEA because they knew they couldn't release without it. Purchasing didn't select incapable suppliers because they knew Sarah would flag them. Operations didn't ramp without proof because they knew the VP would ask "What's your Cp?"

The rules, combined with aligned metrics, had changed behavior. Prevention wasn't something Kristina had to advocate for. It was just how work got done.

Tom knocked on her door. "New sensor program kicked off today. Engineering scheduled DFMEA for next week. Manufacturing and test are already invited."

Kristina smiled. A year ago, she would have had to push for that DFMEA. Now it happened automatically.

"Good," she said. "That's how it should work."

The transformation wasn't complete—they still had 20% COPQ, still had quality issues, still had work to do. But the foundation was solid.

Prevention was becoming the culture. Not completely embedded yet, but moving in the right direction. And culture, once it starts to shift, builds momentum.

The next challenge was taking prevention deeper, not just into organizational structure, but into how they designed products from the start. That work was about to begin.

Chapter 4 — The Blueprint: Planning Quality In, Not Inspecting It Out

Twelve months into the transformation, Kristina got the call she'd been hoping for.

Mark Sullivan, lead engineer on the new infrared sensor program, called her office. "Hey Kristina, we're kicking off design on the Gen-3 sensor. I want to schedule a DFMEA workshop. When can you facilitate?"

Kristina smiled. A year ago, she would have had to chase Mark down and argue for DFMEA. Now he was calling her.

"Let me check," Kristina said, pulling up her calendar. "I can do next Tuesday afternoon. How long do you need?"

"Four hours?" Mark said. "We've got a pretty complex design. Thermal management is tricky, we're using a new seal design, and the connector mounting is tighter than our previous sensors."

"Four hours works. Who's on the team?"

"Me, James from manufacturing, Gary from test, and I was hoping you or Tom could facilitate for quality."

"I'll do it," Kristina said. "Send me the design package by Monday so I can prep. And Mark—thanks for calling. A year ago, you wouldn't have."

Mark laughed. "A year ago, I would've designed it, built it, and hoped nothing would break. Then spent six months fixing field failures. I've learned that four hours of DFMEA beats six months of retrofits."

Monday: Preparation

Kristina spent Monday afternoon reviewing Mark's design package.

The Gen-3 sensor was an evolution of their current surveillance sensor—640×480 infrared detector, stabilized gimbal mount, Ethernet data link. But several things had changed:

New challenges:
- Higher power dissipation (12W vs 8W) due to faster processor

- Operating temperature extended to −40°F to +160°F (vs −20°F to +140°F)
- New elastomer seal (different material, unproven in this application)
- Connector mounted directly to housing (previous design had flex cable isolating vibration)
- Weight reduced 15% (thinner walls, tighter packaging)

Kristina flagged potential failure modes just from reading the specs:
- Thermal: 50% more power in similar volume → overheating risk
- Seal: New material, extreme temperatures → leakage or hardening risk
- Connector: Direct mount, no vibration isolation → stress/fatigue risk
- Housing: Thinner walls → strength/stiffness concerns

She drafted an agenda for the workshop:
DFMEA Workshop Agenda – Gen-3 Sensor
Tuesday, 1:00 PM–5:00 PM, Conference Room B
1. Introductions & DFMEA overview (15 min)
2. System functions review (30 min)
3. Failure modes brainstorming (90 min)
4. Risk assessment – severity, occurrence, detection (60 min)
5. Action planning for high-RPN items (45 min)
6. Next steps & closeout (10 min)

She'd facilitated, a dozen DFMEA workshops over the past year. The key was keeping it structured but not bureaucratic—systematic thinking without getting bogged down in process.

Tuesday: The DFMEA Workshop

The team gathered in Conference Room B at 1:00 PM. Kristina had the whiteboard set up with three columns: *Function | Failure Mode | Effect*

"Thanks for being here," Kristina opened. "We've got four hours to identify what could go wrong with this sensor and figure out how to prevent it. Mark's put a year of design work into this—we want to make sure it succeeds in the field, not just on paper."

She explained the DFMEA process: "We'll work through the sensor systematically. What does it do? How could it fail? What happens if it fails? Why might it fail? How likely? Can we detect it? Then we'll prioritize and fix the high-risk items."

Step 1: Functions (20 minutes)

"Start with the basics," Kristina said. "What does this sensor do?"

The team listed primary functions:
- Capture infrared imagery (640×480, 30 Hz)
- Stabilize line of sight (±0.1° accuracy)
- Transmit data via Ethernet (20 Mbps)
- Operate in environment (−40°F to +160°F, 95% humidity, 20G vibration)
- Mount to gimbal (mechanical + electrical interface)
- Dissipate heat (12W continuous)

"Good," Kristina said. "For each function, we'll ask: how could it fail?"

Step 2: Failure Modes (90 minutes)

Kristina started with the first function. "Infrared imagery—how could that fail?"

The team brainstormed:
- Image quality degraded (blur, noise, dead pixels)
- Frame rate drops below 30 Hz
- Image sensor fails completely
- Optical path gets obstructed or misaligned
- Electronics overheat and shut down

"Let's dig into image quality degraded," Kristina said. "That's pretty broad. What specific failure modes cause that?"

Mark broke it down:
- Lens misalignment (focus shift)
- Detector noise (electronic interference)
- Thermal drift (detector performance degrades at temperature extremes)
- Moisture ingress (condensation on optics)

For each failure mode, Kristina asked: "What causes this and what's the effect?"

Failure Mode: Lens Misalignment

"Why would the lens misalign?" Kristina asked.

James, the manufacturing engineer, jumped in. "Thermal expansion. The lens barrel is aluminum, the housing is aluminum, but they expand at slightly different rates. If we're not careful with the mounting, differential expansion could shift focus."

"What's the effect if focus shifts?" Kristina asked.

"Image goes soft," Mark said. "Not unusable, but reduced sharpness. Operators would complain that targets are harder to identify."

Gary, the test engineer, added: "And it might not show up in room temperature testing. We'd only see it at temperature extremes—minus 40 or plus 160."

Kristina wrote on the whiteboard:

Failure Mode: Lens misalignment (focus shift)

Potential cause: Thermal expansion mismatch between lens barrel and housing

Effect (local): Image sharpness reduced

Effect (system): Target identification impaired

Effect (customer): Mission degraded, operator complaints

Kristina turned to the team. "This is the kind of thing DFMEA catches. If we don't think about thermal expansion now, we find out when the customer deploys in Alaska and calls to say the image is blurry."

They continued through failure modes. After 90 minutes, they'd identified 12 major failure modes:

1. Lens misalignment (thermal expansion)
2. Detector thermal drift (performance at temperature extremes)
3. Moisture ingress (seal failure)
4. Connector stress failure (vibration + thermal cycling)
5. Electronics overheating (insufficient cooling)
6. Gimbal interface binding (tolerance stack-up)
7. Image processor lockup (software/thermal)
8. Power supply failure (thermal stress)
9. Cable routing interference (EMI/signal integrity)
10. Housing structural failure (vibration + reduced wall thickness)
11. Lens contamination (dust/moisture through seal)
12. Mounting screw loosening (vibration)

"Good work," Kristina said. "Now we need to assess risk for each one."

Step 3: Risk Assessment – Severity (30 minutes)

Kristina explained the severity rating: "On a scale of 1 to 10, how bad is the effect if this failure occurs?"

She wrote the scale on the whiteboard:

Severity Scale:
- 1–2: Minor inconvenience, no functional impact
- 3–4: Reduced performance, functional but degraded
- 5–6: Significant performance loss, usability affected
- 7–8: Major loss of function, customer impact
- 9: Safety hazard or mission failure
- 10: Safety hazard with warning

"For each failure mode, assume the failure happens and ask: how bad is it?"

They rated severity for each failure mode:
- Lens misalignment: Severity = 7 (major performance loss, reduced target identification)
- Detector thermal drift: Severity = 8 (unusable at temperature extremes)
- Moisture ingress: Severity = 9 (complete failure, could happen without warning)
- Connector stress failure: Severity = 9 (loss of data, mission failure)
- Electronics overheating: Severity = 8 (system shutdown, mission interruption)

The team debated severity for moisture ingress. Mark argued for 8, Gary argued for 9.

"If the seal fails and moisture gets in," Gary said, "the detector could fail permanently. And we might not know until it happens in the field. That's mission failure without warning. I'd call that a 9."

Mark agreed. "You're right. If this happens on a critical surveillance mission, it's a big deal."

Kristina noted the importance of the discussion. "This is why DFMEA needs cross-functional input. Engineering might rate it differently than test. The debate helps us understand the real impact."

Step 4: Risk Assessment – Occurrence (30 minutes)

"Occurrence rating," Kristina explained. "How likely is this failure to occur? Scale of 1 to 10."

She wrote the scale:

Occurrence Scale:
- 1: Nearly impossible (<1 in 1,000,000)
- 2–3: Very unlikely (1 in 20,000 to 1 in 100,000)
- 4–5: Occasional (1 in 2,000 to 1 in 20,000)
- 6–7: Frequent (1 in 200 to 1 in 2,000)
- 8–9: Very frequent (1 in 20 to 1 in 200)
- 10: Nearly certain (>1 in 20)

"Base this on data if you have it," Kristina said. "Process capability, historical failure rates, similar designs. If you don't have data, use engineering judgment but be conservative."

Lens misalignment (thermal expansion)

"Do we have data on thermal expansion?" Kristina asked.

Mark pulled up calculations. "The lens barrel and housing are both aluminum—same material, same expansion coefficient. But the mounting interface has tolerances. I'm calculating worst-case mismatch of about 0.002 inches over the temperature range."

"Is that enough to shift focus?" Gary asked.

"Depends on the lens design," Mark said. "For this f/1.2 lens, depth of focus is about 0.005 inches. So we're at the edge. I'd say 50/50 whether it causes noticeable focus shift."

Kristina translated: "50/50 means about 1 in 2. That's Occurrence = 9. High."

The team rated occurrence for each failure mode, pulling data where available:

"Moisture ingress (seal failure): Occurrence = 6 (new seal material, unproven; similar seals have 3% field failure rate)

"Connector stress failure: Occurrence = 7 (direct mount with no vibration isolation; previous design with isolation had 0.5% field failure rate)

"Electronics overheating: Occurrence = 5 (thermal modeling shows marginal cooling; 50% chance of exceeding maximum junction temperature)

Step 5: Risk Assessment – Detection (20 minutes)

"Last rating: Detection," Kristina said. "How likely are we to catch this failure before it reaches the customer?"

Detection Scale:
- 1–2: Almost certain (100% inspection or automated detection)

- 3–4: High likelihood (inspection or test catches most)
- 5–6: Moderate (catches some, misses some)
- 7–8: Low (relies on sampling or special testing)
- 9: Very low (no inspection, testing doesn't reveal)
- 10: Cannot detect (failure only occurs in field conditions)

"Think about your test plan," Kristina said. "What testing will catch each failure mode?"

Lens misalignment (thermal):

Gary reviewed the test plan. "We'll do thermal cycling during qualification—minus 40 to plus 160, 50 cycles. We'll take images at temperature extremes and check focus."

"So Detection = 2?" Kristina asked. "You'll definitely catch it?"

"If it happens during thermal cycling, yes," Gary said. "But if the mounting shifts slowly over time—like after 100 cycles instead of 50—we might miss it. I'd say Detection = 3. High likelihood but not certain."

Moisture ingress:

"We'll do humidity chamber testing," Gary said. "1000 hours at 95% humidity, 140°F. If the seal fails during that test, we'll catch it."

"But if it fails after 2000 hours?" James asked.

"Then we won't catch it until the field," Gary admitted. "Detection = 4. Good test, but time-limited."

They rated detection for all failure modes.

Step 6: Calculate Risk Priority Number (10 minutes)

Kristina explained RPN: "Risk priority number equals Severity × Occurrence × Detection. It's a screening tool—higher RPN means higher priority for action."

She calculated RPN for each failure mode:

Failure Modes with RPN:
1. Lens misalignment: S=7, O=9, D=3 → RPN = 189
2. Electronics overheating: S=8, O=5, D=4 → RPN = 160
3. Connector stress failure: S=9, O=7, D=3 → RPN = 189
4. Moisture ingress: S=9, O=6, D=4 → RPN = 216
5. Detector thermal drift: S=8, O=4, D=3 → RPN = 96
6. Gimbal interface binding: S=6, O=5, D=2 → RPN = 60
7. Housing structural failure: S=8, O=3, D=2 → RPN = 48

"Rule of thumb," Kristina said. "RPN over 100 gets an action plan. Over 150 is high priority. Over 200 is critical—we need to address it before design release."

Four failure modes were over 100:
- Moisture ingress: RPN 216
- Lens misalignment: RPN 189
- Connector stress: RPN 189
- Electronics overheating: RPN 160

Step 7: Action Planning (45 minutes)

"Last step," Kristina said. "For each high-RPN item, what are we going to do?"

Moisture Ingress (RPN 216):

"This seal is unproven," Gary said. "Why are we using a new material?"

"Cost reduction," Mark admitted. "The current seal costs $12, this new one costs $8. Program management wanted to reduce BOM cost."

Kristina asked the critical question: "What's the lifecycle cost if the seal fails in the field?"

They calculated:
- Seal replacement: $400 (overnight shipping + handling)
- Field service: $2,400 (technician travel + labor)
- Customer downtime: $8,000 (mission unavailable)
- Total field failure cost: $10,800

"So we save $4 per sensor to use the cheaper seal," Kristina said. "But if it fails in the field, it costs $10,800. At 6% occurrence rate, that's an expected cost of $648 per sensor. The $12 seal is actually cheaper."

Mark saw it immediately. "We should stick with the proven seal. The $4 cost saving isn't worth the $648 risk."

"Action item," Kristina said. "Revert to proven seal material. Expected benefit: Occurrence drops from 6 to 2, RPN drops from 216 to 72."

Lens Misalignment (RPN 189):

"We need to design for thermal expansion," Mark said. "I'm thinking we add a titanium spacer in the lens mount. Titanium has lower thermal expansion than aluminum. We can tune the spacer thickness to compensate for housing expansion."

James asked, "How much does that cost?"

"About $18 in material and machining," Mark said. "But it's added during assembly, no tooling impact."

"And if we don't do it?" Kristina asked.

"Then we risk focus shift at temperature extremes," Gary said. "Which means field failures, customer complaints, and probably a retrofit program. That's $50K–$100K minimum."

"So, $18 per sensor prevents $50K retrofit," Kristina said. "Easy decision."

"Action item," Mark said. "Add titanium compensation spacer to lens mount design. Expected benefit: Occurrence drops from 9 to 2, RPN drops from 189 to 42."

Connector Stress (RPN 189):

"The issue is direct mounting," James said. "Previous design had a flex cable that absorbed vibration. This design mounts the connector directly to the housing. All that 20G vibration goes straight into the connector pins."

"Why did we change it?" Kristina asked.

"Weight reduction," Mark said. "Flex cable added 45 grams. We're trying to hit a weight target."

"What's the failure mode if the connector fails?" Gary asked.

"Loss of data link," Mark said. "Sensor becomes useless."

Kristina did the math: "At 7% occurrence, we're expecting 7 field failures per 100 sensors. That's $75,600 in field service costs to save 45 grams per sensor."

Mark thought about it. "What if we keep the direct mount but add a stress relief feature? Like a flexible boot over the connector that limits bending moment?"

James nodded. "That could work. Costs maybe $5 per sensor, adds 10 grams."

"Much better than 45 grams and flex cable," Mark said. "And way better than field failures."

"Action item," Kristina said. "Add stress relief boot to connector mounting. Expected benefit: Occurrence drops from 7 to 3, RPN drops from 189 to 81."

Electronics Overheating (RPN 160):

"We're at 12W in a smaller volume," Mark said. "Thermal modeling shows junction temperature at 122°C in worst case. Max rating is 125°C. That's too close."

"What are the options?" Kristina asked.

Mark pulled up thermal models. "Three approaches: increase housing size for more heat sink area, add heat pipe for better thermal transfer, or reduce processor speed to lower power."

"How much does each cost?" James asked.

Mark showed the trade-offs:

- Larger housing: Adds 50 grams, violates weight target
- Heat pipe: Adds $45 per sensor, adds 15 grams
- Reduce processor speed: No cost, no weight, but 20% slower image processing

"The customer wants 30 Hz frame rate," Gary said. "If we slow the processor, can we still hit that?"

"Barely," Mark said. "We'd be at 29.5 Hz. Within spec, but no margin."

Kristina asked, "What's the cost if electronics overheat in the field?"

"Complete failure," Gary said. "Sensor dead until replaced. That's $10,800 per occurrence. At 5% occurrence, expected cost is $540 per sensor."

"So heat pipe at $45 prevents $540 in failures," Kristina calculated. "That's 12:1 ROI."

"Heat pipe it is," Mark said. "And it gives us margin, junction temp drops to 105°C, well below the 125°C limit."

"Action item," Kristina said. "Add heat pipe to thermal management design. Expected benefit: Occurrence drops from 5 to 2, RPN drops from 160 to 64."

Step 8: Documentation & Next Steps (10 minutes)
Kristina summarized the workshop results:

DFMEA Summary – Gen-3 Sensor:
- 12 failure modes identified
- 4 high-priority (RPN >100) addressed with design changes:

1. Seal: Use proven material (+$4 per sensor)

2. Lens: Add titanium spacer (+$18 per sensor)

3. Connector: Add stress relief boot (+$5 per sensor)

4. Thermal: Add heat pipe (+$45 per sensor)
- Total BOM impact: +$72 per sensor
- Prevented field failure cost: ~$850 per sensor
- Net value: $778 per sensor

"These changes cost $72 per sensor," Kristina said. "Over a 500-unit program, that's $36K added to BOM cost. But we're preventing an expected $425K in field failures. Net savings: $389K."

Mark looked at the numbers. "A year ago, I would've released this design without DFMEA. We would've saved $36K in BOM cost and spent $425K fixing field failures. DFMEA just prevented a $425K mistake."

"And that's just the direct cost," Gary added. "Doesn't include customer-satisfaction impact, schedule delays, or reputation damage."

Kristina documented next steps:
- Mark: Update design with all four changes (2 weeks)
- Gary: Update test plan to validate changes (1 week)
- James: Update manufacturing work instructions (1 week)
- Kristina: Update DFMEA document, track to closure (ongoing)
- Team: Reconvene in 3 weeks to review updated design

"Good session," Kristina said. "Four hours of DFMEA just saved us six months of retrofits."

Week 3: Design Changes Implemented

Mark spent two weeks implementing the DFMEA-driven changes:
1. Seal material: Reverted to proven elastomer (nitrile vs new silicone)
2. Lens mount: Added titanium compensation spacer (0.025" thick, compensates for thermal expansion)
3. Connector: Added elastomeric stress relief boot (limits bending moment to <5 lb-in)
4. Thermal: Added copper heat pipe (transfers heat from processor to housing)

BOM cost increased by $72 per sensor (from $1,240 to $1,312). Program management initially pushed back. "Why are we adding cost?"

Kristina showed them the DFMEA summary: "$72 prevents $850 in field failures."

The Program Manager approved the changes.

Week 8: Validation Testing

Gary ran environmental validation testing on the updated design:

Thermal Testing: −40°F to +160°F, 100 cycles
- Lens focus: Remained within 0.001" (tight spec: 0.005")
- Electronics: Junction temp peaked at 107°C (spec: 125°C max)

- Result: PASS

Seal Testing: 95% humidity, +160°F, 2000 hours
- Moisture ingress: <0.1 grams (spec: <1 gram)
- Seal integrity maintained throughout test
- Result: PASS

Vibration Testing: 20G RMS, 8 hours per axis
- Connector stress: Measured <4 lb-in (spec: <5 lb-in)
- No fatigue cracks, no loosening
- Result: PASS

Combined Environmental: Thermal + vibration simultaneous
- All functions nominal across full operating range
- Result: PASS

All four high-RPN failure modes validated as prevented.

Month 15: First Deployment

The Gen-3 sensor deployed to customer operations in three environments:
- Arctic surveillance (Alaska, −35°F typical)
- Desert surveillance (Middle East, +155°F typical)
- Maritime surveillance (Pacific, high humidity + vibration)

After 6 months of field deployment (500 sensors, cumulative 36,000 operating hours):
- Field failures: 0
- Customer complaints: 0
- Performance issues: 0

Kristina compared to the previous sensor generation (Gen-2), which had launched 18 months earlier without DFMEA:
- Gen-2 field failures in first 6 months: 12 units (2.4%)
- Gen-2 field service costs: $129,600
- Gen-2 customer complaints: 23 (thermal issues, seal failures, connector problems)

Gen-3 with DFMEA: Zero failures, zero complaints, $129,600 avoided cost.

The $36K invested in BOM cost prevented $129,600 in field failures. ROI: 3.6:1.

And that didn't count the customer satisfaction impact. The customer sent an email to the Aegis CEO:

"The Gen-3 sensor is the most reliable unit we've deployed. Zero failures across three climate zones. We're increasing our follow-on order by 40% and specifying Aegis for two additional programs."

That follow-on order was worth $8.4M.

The Pattern Spreads

Word spread through the engineering department. The Gen-3 DFMEA had prevented field failures that plagued previous programs. Engineers started requesting DFMEA early in design, not as compliance but as risk mitigation.

A radar housing engineer approached Tom: "I heard the sensor team used DFMEA to prevent field failures. Can you facilitate one for our program?"

"Absolutely," Tom said. "When's your design review?"

"Three weeks. I want to do DFMEA before that."

Tom smiled. This was the culture shift they'd been building toward. Engineers weren't waiting to be told—they were asking for prevention.

Over the next six months:
- 8 additional DFMEA workshops conducted
- 47 high-RPN failure modes identified and addressed
- Estimated prevented field failure costs: $1.2M
- Average BOM cost increase: $45 per unit
- **Net savings: $1.15M**

And more importantly: field failure rates across new programs dropped 73%.

Prevention at the Source

Fifteen months into the transformation, Kristina reviewed progress with the VP of operations.

"COPQ is down to $21M, 17.5% of revenue," Kristina reported. "That's a $9M improvement from where we started."

"What's driving it?" the VP asked.

"Design prevention," Kristina said. "DFMEA is catching issues before they're built into products. We're preventing failures instead of fixing them."

She showed him the data:
- Programs with DFMEA: 0.3% field failure rate

- Programs without DFMEA (historical): 2.1% field failure rate
- 87% reduction in field failures for DFMEA programs

"That sensor program—Gen-3—is the proof point," Kristina said. "Four hours of DFMEA, $36K in design changes, zero field failures. The previous sensor without DFMEA had 12 field failures costing $130K, plus customer relationship damage."

"How many programs are using DFMEA now?" the VP asked.

"All new designs," Kristina said. "It's part of the design review process. Engineers can't release without it—and they don't want to. They've seen what happens when you skip it."

The VP nodded. "That sensor customer expanding their order by 40%, that's an $8.4M contract we wouldn't have won if Gen-3 had the same failure rate as Gen-2."

"Exactly," Kristina said. "Quality isn't just preventing cost—it's winning revenue."

The transformation was working, but Kristina knew they weren't done. DFMEA prevented design failures. But what about requirements failures—products that met the spec but missed the customer's actual need?

That problem showed up the following month. And it taught Kristina that preventing failures meant understanding what customers really needed, not just what they specified.

Chapter 5 — The Compass: Understanding Your Customer Isn't a Survey, It's a Strategy

Sixteen months into the transformation, Kristina got the call she'd been dreading.

"Kristina, we've got a situation." It was Jack Morrison, the Program Manager for the tactical radio program. "Customer is reporting failures on the RT-4400 units we delivered last quarter. Five units down, more showing issues. They're threatening to stop deployment."

The RT-4400 was a handheld tactical radio—Aegis's first entry into the portable communications market. They'd delivered 200 units three months ago. Field failures were already at 2.5% and climbing.

"What's failing?" Kristina asked.

"Display shutdowns," Jack said. "Radio keeps working but the screen goes dark. Happens at random, then comes back after it cools down. Customer says it's unacceptable—these are mission-critical comms."

Kristina pulled up the design file. The RT-4400 had gone through DFMEA. She'd been in that workshop. They'd identified thermal risks and addressed them. The design had passed all qualification testing, temperature cycling, humidity, vibration, drop testing.

"We tested this thoroughly," Kristina said. "What's different about how they're using it?"

"I don't know," Jack admitted. "But the customer is furious. Can you figure out what's wrong?"

Kristina grabbed Tom. "Road trip. We're going to see how the customer actually uses these radios."

Day 1: The Customer Visit

Kristina and Tom flew to Fort Bragg to meet with the 82nd Airborne unit using the RT-4400 radios.

Captain Sarah Mills met them at the base. "Thanks for coming. These radios are supposed to be battlefield proven. But we're getting failures that could get people killed."

"Walk us through how you use them," Kristina said.

Captain Mills took them to the training area where a squad was running tactical drills. It was mid-July, North Carolina heat. Temperature was 96°F with high humidity.

The soldiers wore full combat gear—body armor, helmet, load-bearing vest with pouches for ammunition, water, medical supplies. The RT-4400 radio was clipped to the vest, positioned on the chest.

Kristina watched one soldier operating the radio. After 20 minutes of movement, he keyed the mic: "Display's dark again, Sergeant."

The soldier unclipped the radio, held it away from his body. After 30 seconds, the display flickered back on.

"That's what keeps happening," Captain Mills said. "Display shuts down, comes back when they cool it off."

Kristina asked to see the radio. It was hot to the touch—uncomfortably hot.

"How long have they been wearing these?" Tom asked.

"About 90 minutes," Captain Mills said. "They'll wear them 6–8 hours on operations."

Tom pulled out an infrared thermometer and measured the radio housing: 158°F.

Kristina's mind raced. The RT-4400 was spec'd to operate from −4°F to +140°F. They'd tested it at those extremes. But they hadn't tested it at 158°F—because that wasn't in the spec.

"Can we observe more?" Kristina asked.

Over the next two hours, she and Tom watched how the soldiers actually used the radios:

Observation 1: Body Heat Amplification

The radio wasn't operating in 96°F ambient temperature. It was pressed against the soldier's chest, covered by body armor. Body heat (98.6°F) plus solar radiation on black body armor, plus the radio's own power dissipation (2.5W) created a microclimate significantly hotter than ambient.

Tom calculated: "Radio is essentially operating in a 150–160°F environment, not the 96°F ambient we'd assume."

Observation 2: No Airflow

In the lab, they'd tested with the radio on a bench—full airflow around it. In actual use, the radio was sandwiched between body armor and the soldier's chest. Zero airflow. Heat had nowhere to go.

Observation 3: Continuous Operation

56

In the lab, they'd tested with duty cycle—radio on for 30 minutes, off for 30 minutes. In actual use, soldiers kept radios on continuously for 6–8 hours. No thermal recovery time.

Observation 4: Sun Loading

The lab's temperature chamber didn't simulate direct sunlight. In the field, radios were exposed to full solar radiation—adding another 20–30°F of heating.

Kristina had found the gap. The RT-4400 met the specification (operate −4°F to +140°F) but missed the requirement (work reliably in actual combat conditions).

They'd designed to the spec, not to the need.

Day 2: Understanding the Failure

Back at the hotel, Kristina and Tom analyzed what they'd learned.

"The display is shutting down because the LCD controller is hitting thermal shutdown," Tom said. "It's spec'd to a 140°F junction temperature. When the radio housing hits 158°F, the controller is probably at 165–170°F internally. It protects itself by shutting down."

"Why didn't we catch this in testing?" Kristina asked.

Tom pulled up the test plan. "We tested at 140°F ambient, full power, for 8 hours. Radio housing reached 152°F. We were close to the limit but within spec."

"But we tested with airflow," Kristina said. "And we didn't simulate body heat or solar loading."

"Right," Tom said. "We tested the requirement in the specification, not the requirement in actual use."

Kristina called Jack Morrison. "I found the problem. The radio meets the temperature spec but not the temperature reality. Soldiers are using it in hotter conditions than we designed for."

"How much hotter?" Jack asked.

"158–160°F instead of 140°F," Kristina said. "Twenty degrees makes the difference between working and failing."

"Can we fix it?"

"Yes, but we need to understand all the ways they use it first. We're going back tomorrow to observe more scenarios."

Day 3: Use-Case Analysis

Kristina and Tom spent the next day documenting how soldiers used the RT-4400 in different scenarios:

Use Case 1: Mounted Operations (Vehicle)

Radio clipped inside vehicle. Temperature: ambient + solar through window + vehicle heating system. Measured: 135–145°F. No failures observed.

Use Case 2: Dismounted Operations (Open Terrain)

Radio clipped to vest, full sun exposure, moderate activity. Measured: 155–160°F. Display shutdowns observed after 60–90 minutes.

Use Case 3: Dismounted Operations (Heavy Activity)

Radio clipped to vest, full sun, running/climbing/combat drills. Measured: 160–165°F. Display shutdowns within 30–45 minutes.

Use Case 4: Indoor Operations (Building Clearing)

Radio clipped to vest, no direct sun, high activity. Measured: 145–150°F. Marginal—occasional shutdowns after 2–3 hours.

Use Case 5: Cold Weather Operations (Simulation)

Radio clipped to vest, winter gear. Not currently tested but Captain Mills mentioned they'd deploy to Alaska. Specification: −4°F. Concern: Would battery perform? Would LCD remain functional at extreme cold?

Kristina documented the environmental requirements based on actual use:

Current Spec: −4°F to +140°F ambient

Actual Use Environment:

- Cold extreme: −20°F (Alaska winter operations)
- Hot extreme: +165°F (desert + body heat + sun + high activity)
- Humidity: Up to 95% (jungle operations)
- Submersion: Radio sometimes submerged in water during river crossings
- Vibration/shock: Higher than test spec (soldiers running, dropping equipment)

The specification reflected what someone thought soldiers would encounter. The actual use revealed what soldiers really experienced.

Week 2: Translating Needs to Requirements

Back at Aegis, Kristina gathered the RT-4400 team—Mark Sullivan (now designing tactical equipment), James Chen (manufacturing), and Gary Santos (test).

"We have a gap between specification and reality," Kristina said. She showed them photos and temperature data from Fort Bragg.

"The customer specified 140°F maximum operating temperature. They didn't specify 'clipped to body armor in desert sun during high-activity operations.' But that's how they use it."

Mark looked at the data. "How were we supposed to know they'd use it that way?"

"By asking," Kristina said. "We assumed how they'd use it. We should have observed."

She explained the concept of Voice of Customer: "VOC means understanding what the customer actually needs, not just what they specify. Specifications are often incomplete or based on assumptions. We need to capture the real need."

The VOC Process Kristina Proposed:

Step 1: Interview Actual Users (Not Just Buyers)
- Talk to soldiers who carry the radio, not just procurement officers
- Ask: "Tell me about a time the radio failed you." (not "Do you like the radio?")
- Ask: "What's the harshest environment you've used it in?"
- Ask: "If you could change one thing, what would it be?"

Step 2: Observe Actual Use
- Visit field operations, not just demos
- Watch how they use it in real conditions
- Measure actual environment (temperature, humidity, shock)
- Document edge cases and worst-case scenarios

Step 3: Translate Needs to Measurable Requirements
- Customer need: "Reliable in all combat conditions"
- Engineering requirement: "Operate −20°F to +165°F housing temperature, 95% humidity, 40G shock, 3-foot drop onto concrete, submersion to 3 feet for 30 minutes"
- Validation criteria: "Test in simulated combat conditions (body heat, solar loading, continuous operation)"

Step 4: Test in Actual Conditions
- Don't just test to specification limits
- Test to actual use conditions

- Include combined stresses (heat + humidity + vibration simultaneously)
- Use actual mounting configurations (chest-mounted, not bench-mounted)

"If we'd done VOC before designing the RT-4400," Kristina said, "we would have known about body heat, solar loading, and continuous operation. We would have designed for 165°F, not 140°F."

Week 3: The Retrofit

The immediate problem: 200 radios in the field, more shutting down daily.

Mark analyzed thermal paths. "The bottleneck is here." He pointed to the LCD controller. "It's on the main circuit board with the processor, which generates most of the heat. No thermal isolation."

"What are the options?" Kristina asked.

Mark outlined three approaches:

Option 1: Add External Heat Sink
- Bolt aluminum heat sink to housing
- Improves heat dissipation 30%
- Cost: $45 per unit
- Implementation: Field retrofit possible

Option 2: Relocate LCD Controller
- Move LCD controller to separate board, thermally isolated from processor
- Improves thermal margin significantly (controller runs 25°F cooler)
- Cost: $180 per unit (requires board redesign + rework)
- Implementation: Requires return to factory

Option 3: Upgrade LCD Controller
- Use higher-temperature-rated component (rated to 165°F vs 140°F)
- Direct fix to root cause
- Cost: $28 per unit (component swap)
- Implementation: Requires return to factory

"What's the best solution?" Jack asked.

Kristina did the lifecycle cost analysis:

Option 1 (Heat Sink): $45 × 200 = $9,000
- Pros: Quick, field-installable
- Cons: Only 30% improvement—might not be enough in worst cases

Option 2 (Relocate Controller): $180 × 200 = $36,000
- Pros: Significant improvement
- Cons: Expensive, long retrofit timeline

Option 3 (Upgrade Controller): $28 × 200 = $5,600
- Pros: Directly addresses root cause, lowest cost
- Cons: Requires factory return (2 weeks per unit)

"We should do Option 3," Kristina said. "It fixes the root cause for the lowest cost. And we implement Option 1 as interim fix, add heat sinks in the field so radios can operate while we schedule factory upgrades."

"Total retrofit cost: $9,000 (heat sinks) + $5,600 (controller upgrades) = $14,600"

Jack approved the plan. But the question hung in the room: "Why didn't we design this correctly the first time?"

"Because we didn't do VOC," Kristina said. "We designed to a specification without understanding the actual use. This is a requirements failure, not a design failure."

Week 6: The Fix + The Prevention

The retrofit proceeded:
- Weeks 1–2: Install heat sinks at Fort Bragg (radios remain operational)
- Weeks 3–6: Return radios in batches to Aegis for controller upgrade
- Week 7: All radios upgraded and redeployed

Field results after upgrade:
- Operating environment: −10°F to +165°F (actual measured)
- Display shutdowns: Zero over next 3 months
- Customer satisfaction: "Problem resolved, confidence restored."

But Kristina knew the real work was prevention—making sure this didn't happen on future programs.

She created a VOC checklist for all new product development:
VOC Checklist – Required Before Design Release
Customer/User Engagement:

☐ Interview at least 3 actual users (not just buyers)

☐ Observe product use in field environment (not just lab)

☐ Document worst-case scenarios (environmental, usage, operational)

☐ Identify edge cases (unusual but important use cases)

Use Case Analysis:

☐ List all intended use cases

☐ For each use case, document actual environment (temperature, humidity, shock, chemical exposure)

☐ Measure actual conditions (don't assume—measure)

☐ Identify combined stresses (heat + humidity + vibration together)

Requirements Translation:

☐ Translate customer needs into measurable engineering requirements

☐ Include margin for worst case (spec + 20% for thermal, +2× for mechanical shock)

☐ Define validation criteria (how will we prove this meets the need?)

Validation Testing:

☐ Test in actual use configuration (not just bench test)

☐ Test combined stresses, not just individual stresses

☐ Test continuous operation, not just duty cycle

☐ Include actual mounting, actual airflow restrictions, actual environmental loading

"This checklist becomes part of design review," Kristina told the team. "Before any design is released, we verify VOC is complete. If you haven't talked to users and observed field use, you're not ready to design."

Month 18: VOC Becomes Standard Practice

Over the next three months, VOC became embedded in Aegis' design process.

Example 1: Gimbal System for Maritime Use

Engineer submitted design for review. Kristina asked: "Did you do VOC?"

"Yes," the engineer said. "Specification says salt-spray resistance per MIL-STD-810. We designed to that."

"Did you visit a ship and observe actual use?" Kristina asked.

"No, but the spec covers it."

"Go visit," Kristina said. "Then come back and tell me if the spec is complete."

The engineer visited a destroyer. He found:
- Salt spray test in lab: intermittent mist, 24-hour exposure
- Actual shipboard environment: continuous salt spray + standing saltwater + direct sun + high humidity + diesel exhaust + cleaning chemicals

He redesigned the gimbal with enhanced sealing and corrosion-resistant coatings. Cost: $120 per unit more than original design. Prevented failures that would have cost $8,000 per retrofit.

"VOC just saved us $160,000 on a 20-unit program," he reported.

Example 2: Sensor for Arctic Operations

Customer specified −40°F operation. Engineer asked: "Should I visit them in Alaska to observe?"

"Yes," Kristina said. "Specification is one data point. Reality is what matters."

The engineer spent three days at a forward operating base in Alaska. He learned:
- Battery performance at −40°F: not in spec (chemistry degrades below −20°F)
- Touchscreen operation: impossible with gloves (soldiers can't remove gloves in −40°F)
- Connector mating: freezing made connectors difficult to disconnect
- Shock: handling while cold-soaked made housing brittle

He updated the design:
- Heater circuit for battery (maintains operating temperature)
- Physical buttons instead of touchscreen-only interface
- Connector with positive lock (prevents freezing/binding)

- Housing material changed to maintain ductility at low temperature

Cost impact: $85 per sensor. Prevented field failures: estimated 15% of fleet (30 units × $6,000 = $180,000).

"VOC doesn't cost money," the engineer said. "It saves money by preventing expensive mistakes."

Month 18: Progress Review

Kristina reviewed progress with the VP of operations.

"COPQ is down to $19M, 16% of revenue," she reported. "That's an $11M improvement from start."

"What's the breakdown?" the VP asked.

"Design prevention through DFMEA is the big driver," Kristina said. "But VOC is catching a different category—requirement failures. Products that meet spec but miss the need."

She showed the data:

Field Failures by Root Cause (Historical):
- Design defects: 45% (addressed by DFMEA)
- Manufacturing defects: 30% (addressed by process control)
- Requirement gaps: 25% (addressed by VOC)

Field Failures After DFMEA + VOC:
- Design defects: down 87% (DFMEA catching design issues)
- Requirement gaps: down 73% (VOC catching spec gaps)
- Total field failure rate: 2.1% → 0.5% (76% reduction)

"The RT-4400 radio problem cost us $14,600 to retrofit," Kristina said. "If we'd done VOC before designing, we would have spec'd for 165°F instead of 140°F. Cost difference in initial design: maybe $8 per unit, or $1,600 total. We spent $14,600 fixing a problem that would have cost $1,600 to prevent."

"That's a 9:1 cost ratio," the VP calculated.

"Exactly. And that's just direct cost. Doesn't count the customer relationship damage or the deployment delay."

The VP nodded. "I'm seeing a pattern. Every prevention investment is 10 to 50 times cheaper than fixing failures later."

"That's the fundamental economics of quality," Kristina said. "Prevention costs are measured in hundreds or thousands. Failure costs are measured in tens or hundreds of thousands."

She paused. "However, we're still not done. DFMEA prevents design failures. VOC prevents requirement failures. We still have manufacturing failures. Defects that happen on the production floor, not in the design."

"What's the solution?" the VP asked.

"Operator empowerment," Kristina said. "Getting the people who build the product to own quality, not just defer to inspection. That's the next phase."

Chapter Close: Beyond Specifications

Eighteen months into the transformation, Kristina reflected on what they'd learned.

DFMEA taught them to think through how designs could fail. VOC taught them to understand what customers actually needed.

Both were forms of prevention, stopping problems before they happened. But they required different mindsets.

DFMEA was technical: What could fail? Why? How likely? VOC was human: What does the customer really need? How do they actually use it?

The RT-4400 radio had been a painful lesson. They'd met every specification but missed the fundamental need: work reliably as soldiers' lives depend on it.

Engineering had designed to assumptions. VOC forced them to design to reality.

And reality, Kristina learned, was always more complex than assumptions.

The soldier wearing body armor in 96°F heat wasn't operating in 96°F—he was operating in 160°F. The specification said 140°F. Reality said 160°F.

Specifications were negotiated between buyers and sellers. Reality was what happened when people actually used the product.

VOC closed that gap.

But Kristina knew the transformation still had a long way to go. They'd fixed design and requirements. Next, they had to fix manufacturing—the place where good designs turned into defective products because of how they were built.

That work started the following month.

Chapter 6 — The Human Factor: Building a Culture Where People Stop the Line

Nineteen months into the transformation, Kristina faced a problem she'd been avoiding.

DFMEA was preventing design failures. VOC was preventing requirement failures. But manufacturing defects? Parts were being built wrong despite good designs, and they still accounted for 35% of their quality costs.

Line 3, the avionics assembly line, was the worst offender. First pass yield stuck at 89%. Every week, 11% of output needed rework. The inspectors caught the defects, but only after operators had already built them.

Tom knocked on Kristina's office door. "Line 3 rejected another batch. Twenty housings with incorrect torque on the mounting screws. Third time this month."

Kristina pulled up the data. Line 3 had four chronic issues:

1. Mounting screws over-torqued or under-torqued (happens 8% of the time)
2. Connector pins inserted backwards (2% of the time)
3. Thermal compound application inconsistent (4% of the time)
4. Wire routing incorrect (5% of the time)

Total defect rate: 19%. because multiple units had multiple defects, first pass yield was 89%.

Kristina had tried: process documentation, operator training, and more frequent inspection. Nothing stuck. The same problems kept happening.

"I need to spend time on the floor," Kristina told Tom. "I'm missing something."

Day 1: Watching the Line

Kristina arrived at Line 3 at 6:00 AM for first shift. She grabbed a stool and sat at the end of the line, watching.

Line 3 assembled avionics housings—the boxes that contained circuit boards, connectors, and cooling hardware. Eight operators, eight stations, 15-minute cycle time.

Station 1 (Maria): Install circuit board, connect ribbon cables

Station 2 (James): Install connector panel, torque mounting screws

Station 3 (Linda): Apply thermal compound, install cooling plate

Station 4 (Carlos): Route power cables through strain relief

Station 5 (Angela): Install top cover, torque fasteners

Station 6 (Robert): Install interface connectors

Station 7 (Susan): Visual inspection

Station 8 (Mike): Functional test, apply serial number

Kristina watched James at Station 2. He was torquing the mounting screws with a manual torque wrench. Specification: 45 in-lbs ±5 in-lbs.

She watched him complete five units. On the third unit, she noticed he struggled to reach the back screws—the fixture blocked easy access. He had to angle the wrench awkwardly.

On the fifth unit, James stopped. He looked at the torque wrench, looked at the housing, then continued.

After the shift, Kristina approached James. "I saw you hesitate on that last unit. What happened?"

James glanced around. "The torque wrench didn't click. I think I'm under torque."

"Did you report it?"

"No."

"Why not?"

James lowered his voice. "Because if I stop the line, I get in trouble for missing quota. Last time I flagged an issue, my supervisor said, 'Just build to the print and let inspection catch it.' So that's what I do."

Kristina felt a pit in her stomach. The operator knew there was a problem but didn't speak up because he'd been told not to.

"What other problems do you see?" Kristina asked.

James hesitated, then: "The fixture is worn. When I place the housing, it shifts about an eighth inch. That makes the back screws hard to reach. I mentioned it two months ago. Nothing happened."

"Anything else?"

"The torque wrench feels loose. I'm not sure it's calibrated. But I don't want to slow the line down to check it."

Kristina spent the rest of the week talking to operators at each station.

Linda (Station 3 – Thermal Compound): "The syringe sometimes dispenses too much, sometimes too little. I try to eyeball it. But I know some units get too much and some don't get enough. Inspection catches the really bad ones."

Carlos (Station 4 – Cable Routing): "The wire routing instruction is confusing. There are three different cable types and they're supposed to go through different strain reliefs. I mix them up sometimes. If inspection doesn't catch it, it gets through."

Angela (Station 5 – Top Cover): "I see defects from earlier stations when I install the cover. Cables not routed right, thermal compound smeared. But I'm not supposed to stop the line. I'm supposed to build my station and move on."

The pattern was clear: "Operators saw problems but didn't report them because they were measured on output, not quality."

Week 2: The Root Cause

Kristina gathered the Line 3 supervisor and the Operations Manager in a conference room.

"I spent a week on Line 3," Kristina said. "I found the root cause of our quality problems."

The supervisor bristled. "My operators are trained. They follow the work instructions."

"Your operators are trying," Kristina said. "But they're set up to fail. Let me show you what I learned."

She laid out the problems:

Problem 1: Fixture Drift
- Station 2 fixture worn, housing shifts 1/8
- Makes back screws hard to access
- Operators compensate by angling torque wrench
- Results in inconsistent torque
- Reported 2 months ago, not fixed

Problem 2: Tool Calibration
- Torque wrench feels loose (operator observation)
- No regular calibration schedule
- Operators don't have authority to pull tools for calibration

Problem 3: Thermal Compound Dispenser
- Syringe application inconsistent
- No measurement tool
- Operators eyeball the amount
- Some units get too much, some too little

Problem 4: Cable Routing Instruction
- Work instruction unclear (3 cable types, 3 routing paths)
- Operators mix them up
- No error-proofing to prevent wrong routing

Problem 5: Cultural Issue
- Operators measured solely on output quota
- Stopping line for quality issues discouraged
- "Let inspection catch it" mentality
- Operators see defects from upstream stations but don't speak up

"Here's the real problem," Kristina said. "Your operators know about these issues. They see defects being built. But they don't stop the line because they've been told not to. Quality becomes inspection's problem, not everyone's problem."

The Operations Manager was defensive. "We have to hit production quotas. If operators stop the line every time something looks wrong, we'll never make output."

"You're making output," Kristina said. "But 11% of it is defective. That means we rework 11% of everything we build. That's wasted labor, wasted time, wasted material."

She showed the cost:
- Line 3 output: 1,200 units/month
- Defect rate: 11% (132 units/month)
- Rework cost: $240/unit (4 hours labor × $60/hour)
- Monthly rework cost: 132 × $240 = $31,680
- Annual rework cost: **$380,160**

"That's the cost of telling operators, 'Don't stop the line,'" Kristina said. "We could fix the fixture for $8,000, buy three new torque wrenches for $3,000, design error-proof cable routing for $5,000, and train operators on quality ownership for $2,000. Total: $18,000. We'd save $380K per year."

The Operations Manager was quiet. Then: "What do you propose?"

Week 3: The Plan

Kristina proposed five changes to Line 3:
1. Fix the Physical Problems
"Replace worn fixture" ($8,000)

- New fixture with tighter tolerances
- Housing sits stable, no shift

"Calibrate/replace torque wrenches" ($3,000)
- Send existing wrenches for calibration
- Buy one backup wrench
- Implement monthly calibration check

"Install thermal compound dispenser with measurement" ($4,500)
- Replace manual syringe with metered dispenser
- Set to 2.5 grams ±0.2 grams
- Visual indicator (green = correct, red = out of range)

"Error-proof cable routing" ($5,000)
- Design color-coded strain reliefs (red cable → red relief, blue → blue, yellow → yellow)
- Physically prevents wrong cable in wrong relief (different sizes, keyed connectors)

2. Train Operators on Basic Inspection
"Operators need to know what good looks like," Kristina said. "Not just 'torque to 45 in-lbs' but 'here's what happens if you don't.'"
Training curriculum:
- Why torque matters (over-torque cracks housing, under-torque causes vibration failure)
- How to spot thermal compound problems (too much squeezes out, too little leaves gaps)
- How to verify cable routing (correct colors in correct reliefs)
- How to use torque wrenches properly (angle, technique, reading the click)
- 2-hour training session for each operator, hands-on practice with actual parts.

3. Give Operators Authority to Stop the Line
"This is the culture change," Kristina said. "Operators need permission, actual permission, to stop the line when they see problems."
New rule: "Any operator can stop the line if they see a quality issue. No questions, no penalties."
Response procedure:

1. Operator sees issue → Presses stop button (red button installed at each station)
2. Supervisor notified immediately (light flashes, alarm sounds)
3. Supervisor comes to station: "What did you see?"
4. Team investigates: "Is this a defect? What caused it?"
5. Fix problem or determine if unit can continue
6. Thank operator for catching issue: "Good catch. Thank you for protecting quality."

4. Change Metrics

"Right now, operators are measured on output only," Kristina said. "That needs to change."

New metrics:

- Output (60% of evaluation): Units built per shift
- First pass yield (40% of evaluation): Percentage of units that pass inspection without rework

"This makes operators accountable for quality outcomes, not just quantity," Kristina said. "If they build 100 units but 20 need rework, their first pass yield is 80%. They get credit for building right the first time."

5. Weekly Team Huddles

"Every Friday, 15 minutes," Kristina said. "Team huddle. What problems did you see this week? What do we need to fix?"

Format:

- Each operator shares one observation
- Team discusses: "Is this a pattern? Do we need to fix something?"
- Supervisor documents issues, tracks action items
- Next week: follow-up on last week's issues

"This makes problem-solving a team sport," Kristina said. "Not blame, not finger-pointing. Just continuous improvement."

Week 4: Implementation

Kristina, Tom, and the Line 3 supervisor, Dave, implemented the changes.

Day 1–2: Physical Fixes

- New fixture installed, housing sits stable
- Torque wrenches calibrated, backup wrench added

- Thermal compound dispenser installed with green/red indicator
- Cable routing color-coded, keyed connectors prevent wrong inserting

Day 3: Training
- 8 operators, 2-hour sessions each
- Hands-on practice: "Here's correct torque. Here's over-torque—feel the difference?"
- "Here's correct thermal compound amount. Here's too much, here's too little."
- "Here's correct cable routing. Try putting the wrong cable in the wrong relief—see, it won't fit."

Day 4: The First Test
The line restarted. Everyone knew the new rule: operators could stop the line for quality issues.

At 10:30 AM, the line stopped. Red light flashing, alarm sounding.

James at Station 2 had pressed the button.

Dave rushed over. "What's wrong?"

James held up the housing. "Torque wrench didn't click on this screw. I think I'm under torque."

Dave checked the screw with a backup wrench. "Under torque—35 in-lbs instead of 45 in-lbs."

"Good catch," Dave said loudly, so everyone could hear. "You just prevented a defect from moving downstream. Thank you."

Dave took the housing to rework, gave James a fresh housing. Line restarted.

At lunch, Dave called a quick team meeting. "James stopped the line this morning. That's exactly what we want. He caught a problem before it became a defect. That's protecting quality. Anyone who sees an issue—stop the line. No penalties, no problems. Just stop and we'll figure it out together."

The culture shift had begun.

Week 6: Early Results

Two weeks after implementing the changes, the data started shifting:

Line stops: 8 stops in two weeks (average 4 per week)
- Week 1: 6 stops (operators testing whether it's really okay)

- Week 2: 2 stops (problems decreasing)

Reasons for stops:
- Torque wrench not clicking (2 stops) → Wrench re-calibrated
- Thermal compound dispenser jammed (1 stop) → Dispenser cleared
- Housing arrived with dent from previous operation (1 stop) → Upstream station corrected
- Cable routing unclear for new variant (1 stop) → Work instruction updated
- Connector pins didn't seat fully (1 stop) → Connector issue escalated to engineering
- Fixture loose (2 stops) → Fixture tightened, maintenance added to daily checks

First pass yield progression:
- Week 0 (baseline): 89%
- Week 1 (after fixes): 91%
- Week 2: 93%
- Week 3: 94%
- Week 4: 95%
- Week 6: 96%

Rework costs:
- Baseline: 132 defects/month × $240 = $31,680/month
- Week 6: 48 defects/month × $240 = $11,520/month
- Savings: $20,160/month = **$241,920/year**

The $18,000 investment paid back in less than one month.

But the numbers didn't capture the cultural shift. Operators were engaged. They asked questions. They pointed out problems. They suggested improvements.

Angela: "The thermal compound dispenser is great. But could we move it closer to the work area? I'm reaching too far."

Carlos: "The cable color coding works. But the yellow and green cables look similar under the lights. Could we use red, blue, and orange instead?"

Linda: "I noticed the fixture mounting bolts are loosening after about 200 cycles. Can we add a calibration check every shift?"

These weren't complaints. They were improvements. The operators were thinking about quality, not just building to prints.

Week 8: Scaling the Approach

The Line 3 success spread. Other lines wanted the same changes.

Line 5 (radar assembly): "Can we get error-proofing on our connector panel? We have the same backwards-insertion problem."

Line 7 (gimbal systems): "Our fixture is worn too. Can we get that fixed?"

Line 2 (sensor integration): "Can you train our operators on quality? We want the same authority to stop the line."

Kristina and Tom spent the next month assessing each line, identifying chronic issues, implementing poka-yoke and operator empowerment.

Common patterns across all lines:
1. Worn fixtures causing positioning errors
2. Unclear work instructions leading to variation
3. Manual processes that should be error-proofed
4. Operators seeing problems but not reporting them
5. Metrics focused on output, not first pass yield

Common solutions:
1. Replace/repair worn fixturing ($40K total across 6 lines)
2. Error-proof where possible (keyed connectors, color coding, sensors)
3. Train operators on quality (what good looks like, why it matters)
4. Authority to stop line (red buttons, response procedure)
5. Change metrics (60% output, 40% first pass yield)

Month 21: Progress Review

Twenty-one months into the transformation, Kristina reviewed manufacturing quality with the VP of Operations.

"COPQ is down to $16M, 13% of revenue," Kristina reported. "That's a $14M improvement from where we started."

She broke down the sources:

COPQ reduction by category:
- Design prevention (DFMEA): $5.2M savings
- Requirements prevention (VOC): $2.8M savings
- Manufacturing prevention (Operator empowerment + poka-yoke): $6.0M savings

"Manufacturing was our biggest opportunity," Kristina said. "We were building defects every day, then paying to rework them. Operator empowerment stopped that."

First pass yield improvements:
- Line 2: 86% → 94% (8 points)
- Line 3: 89% → 96% (7 points)
- Line 5: 91% → 97% (6 points)
- Line 7: 84% → 93% (9 points)
- Average across all lines: 87% → 95% (8 points)

Rework cost reduction:
- Baseline: $1.2M/year (all lines)
- Current: $360K/year
- Savings: $840K/year

Investment:
- Physical fixes (fixtures, tools, error-proofing): $68K
- Training (operator quality training): $12K
- Total: $80K
- Payback: 5 weeks

"The financial case is clear," Kristina said. "But the real change is cultural."

She showed the VP a chart: "Operator-Initiated Line Stops"
- Month 1 (implementation): 24 stops
- Month 2: 16 stops
- Month 3: 8 stops
- Month 4: 4 stops
- Month 5–6: 2–3 stops/month (steady state)

"Line stops went down because problems went down," Kristina explained. "In Month 1, operators were catching all the built-in defects. By Month 5, most chronic issues were fixed. Now they only stop for true anomalies—which is exactly what we want."

The VP asked, "Are operators still engaged, or did they go back to old habits?"

"Engaged," Kristina said. "Weekly huddles have generated 47 improvement ideas in the past three months. Operators suggest poka-yoke, process improvements, tool modifications. Eighteen of those ideas have been implemented."

She showed examples of operator suggestions:

- Add go/no-go gauge for connector insertion depth →
  Implemented, prevents incomplete insertion
- Color-code torque wrenches by torque setting →
  Implemented, prevents using wrong wrench
- Add mirror to Station 6 to see hidden connector pins →
  Implemented, easier inspection

"Operators aren't just building units," Kristina said. "They're improving the process. That's the culture we want."

Twenty-one months into the transformation, Kristina reflected on what had changed.

In the beginning, quality was inspection's job. Operators built to prints, inspectors caught defects, rework fixed mistakes.

Now, quality was everyone's job. Operators caught problems before they became defects. Engineers designed for manufacturability. Suppliers delivered capable parts.

The Line 3 transformation had been the proof point. Operators weren't the problem—they were the solution. They saw problems every day. But they needed three things:

1. Authority: Permission to stop the line without penalty
2. Capability: Training on what good looked like and why it mattered
3. Systems: Error-proofing that made mistakes impossible or obvious

Once they had those three things, they took ownership.

James at Station 2 didn't just torque screws anymore. He checked fixture condition, verified torque wrench calibration, and stopped the line if something felt wrong.

Angela at Station 5 didn't just install covers. She inspected upstream work, caught thermal compound issues before they got sealed in, and suggested process improvements.

Carlos at Station 4 didn't just route cables. He proposed the color-coding system that prevented 90% of routing errors.

The operators had become quality owners.

But Kristina knew there was still work to do. Manufacturing quality was improving, but 35% of their remaining defects came from suppliers. Good designs, good manufacturing, but supplier parts that didn't meet specs.

That problem required a different approach—not fixing internal processes, but developing external partners.

That work started the following month.

Chapter 7 — The Extended Factory: Your Quality Is Only as Good as Your Weakest Supplier

Twenty-one months into the transformation, Kristina faced the last major source of quality problems.

Internal manufacturing was under control. First pass yield was 95% across all lines. Operators owned quality. Rework costs had dropped from $1.2M to $360K per year. However, supplier defects remained stubbornly high.

Sarah walked into Kristina's office with a stack of nonconformance reports. "This week's supplier issues: machined brackets out of tolerance, circuit boards with cold solder joints, fasteners with incorrect plating, elastomer seals with dimensional variation."

Kristina reviewed the reports. Twenty-two supplier nonconformances in one week. That meant inspection time, sorting time, expediting replacements, line delays while waiting for good parts.

"How much time are we spending on this?" Kristina asked.

Sarah pulled up the data. "Last month, we spent 240 hours on supplier quality issues. That's 60% of our available time. Tom and I are basically full-time supplier firefighters."

Kristina did the math. 240 hours × $65/hour (loaded rate) = $15,600 per month just in quality engineering time. That didn't count inspection time, material handlers sorting parts, production delays, or expediting costs.

"We're treating symptoms," Kristina said. "Inspection catches supplier defects, but it doesn't prevent them. We need to fix this at the source."

She thought back to the seal supplier project eighteen months ago. They'd visited Precision Seals, assessed their process capability, and co-invested in automated temperature control. Defect rate dropped from 3% to 0.6%.

That was one supplier, one component. Aegis had 28 active suppliers. Kristina needed a systematic approach.

Week 1: Supplier Segmentation

Kristina, Tom, and Sarah spent a week categorizing all 28 suppliers based on three factors:

1. Criticality: How important is this component? Single source? High value? Safety-critical?
2. Performance: What's their current defect rate? Delivery performance? Responsiveness?
3. Complexity: How difficult is their process? How much capability investment would help?

They created a simple matrix:

STRATEGIC SUPPLIERS (High Criticality + Worth Investment):

These suppliers provided critical components, often single-source, where investment in capability would have high ROI.

1. "Precision Seals" (elastomer seals) – Already developed, defect rate 0.6%
2. "Apex Machining" (aluminum housings) – Critical, high volume, current defect rate 4.2%
3. "TechBoard Electronics" (circuit boards) – High complexity, strategic technology, defect rate 3.8%
4. "ConnectorCorp" (mil-spec connectors) – Safety-critical, limited alternate sources, defect rate 5.1%
5. "Optical Systems Inc" (lens assemblies) – High value, specialized, defect rate 2.9%

CAPABLE SUPPLIERS (Good Performance + Maintain):

These suppliers delivered consistent quality. They needed monitoring and periodic audits but not active development.

Fifteen suppliers in this category, average defect rate 0.8%, delivery performance >95%.

PROBLEMATIC SUPPLIERS (High Defects + Need Action):

These suppliers had chronic quality or delivery issues. They needed either development or replacement.

1. "Standard Fasteners" (screws, bolts) – 6.2% defect rate, frequent delivery delays
2. "ElectroPlate Services" (plating/finishing) – 8.1% defect rate, inconsistent coating thickness
3. "Generic Machining" (low-value brackets) – 7.4% defect rate, poor process control
4. "Coast Castings" (aluminum castings) – 5.8% defect rate, porosity issues
5. "ValueBoard" (simple circuit boards) – 9.2% defect rate, quality system immature

6. "Industrial Coatings" (protective coatings) – 4.9% defect rate, process instability
7. "BasicStamp" (metal stampings) – 6.7% defect rate, dimensional variation
8. "CheapConnectors" (commercial connectors) – 7.8% defect rate, contact resistance issues

"Our strategy," Kristina said, "is focus on strategic suppliers first. That's where we'll get the biggest return. Develop capable suppliers through normal monitoring. For problematic suppliers, we either develop them if they're worth it, or replace them if they're not."

Week 2: Site Assessment – Apex Machining

Sarah scheduled site visits to the five strategic suppliers. First visit: Apex Machining.

Apex supplied machined aluminum housings, critical structural components for multiple programs. Current defect rate: 4.2%. Main issues: dimensional out-of-tolerance (2.8%), surface finish problems (1.1%), burrs/sharp edges (0.3%).

Kristina and Sarah arrived at Apex's facility in Southern California. Tom Davis, Apex's owner, met them nervously. "I know we've had quality issues. We're trying to improve."

"That's why we're here," Kristina said. "We want to help you improve. Can you walk us through your process?"

Tom showed them the machining floor. Apex had 12 CNC machines—a mix of newer 4-axis machines and older 3-axis machines. The newer machines were busy on automotive work (Apex's larger customer). The older machines ran Aegis parts.

Observation 1: Equipment Condition

Sarah examined one of the older machines running Aegis housings. The machine was well-maintained but showed age—15 years old, manual tool offset adjustment, no automatic in-process measurement.

"How do you ensure dimensional accuracy?" Sarah asked the operator.

"I measure every tenth part," the operator said. "If it drifts, I adjust the tool offset manually."

"How often does it drift?"

"Every 50–100 parts. The spindle has some runout—about 0.002 inches. I compensate by adjusting offsets."

Sarah documented: "Equipment capability limited by spindle runout. Manual offset adjustment introduces variation. No SPC to detect trends early."

Observation 2: Process Capability

Sarah asked to see process capability data. Tom Davis pulled up a folder. "We ran a capability study six months ago."

The study showed Cp = 1.15 for critical dimensions. Barely capable, predicting 2–3% defect rate, which matched actual performance.

"Why is Cp only 1.15?" Sarah asked.

Tom explained: "The older machines have positional tolerance of ±0.0015 inches. The print tolerance is ±0.005 inches. That gives us theoretical Cp of 1.67. But actual capability is lower because of spindle runout, thermal drift, and tool wear between measurements."

Sarah documented: "Actual capability (Cp 1.15) lower than equipment capability (Cp 1.67) due to process instability."

Observation 3: Inspection Strategy

"You're inspecting every tenth part," Sarah said. "What happens between inspections?"

"We're making bad parts," the operator admitted. "If the process drifts at part 5 and I don't measure until part 10, parts 6–9 might be out of spec."

Sarah calculated: At 4.2% defect rate, roughly 1 in 24 parts was defective. With inspection every tenth part, defects weren't detected until 2–5 bad parts were made.

Sarah documented: "Inspection frequency inadequate to catch drift before defects occur. Need SPC with tighter monitoring."

Observation 4: Culture & Training

Sarah talked to three operators. All were experienced machinists—10+ years each. But none had formal training in SPC, Cp/Cpk, or statistical thinking.

"When you see the process drifting, what do you do?" Sarah asked.

"Adjust the offset," the operator said. "Sometimes I overcorrect, then have to adjust back. It's trial and error."

Sarah documented: "Operators skilled but lack statistical process-control training. Adjusting without SPC charts leads to overcontrol and increased variation."

Week 3: Development Plan – Apex Machining

Back at Aegis, Sarah and Kristina built a development plan for Apex.

Root Causes of 4.2% Defect Rate:

1. Spindle runout on older machines (0.002") reduces capability
2. Manual offset adjustment adds variation
3. Inspection every 10 parts misses drift
4. No SPC to detect trends early
5. Operators lack training on statistical process control

Development Plan:

1. Upgrade Spindle on Two Critical Machines ($35K)

   - Replace worn spindles on two machines running highest-volume Aegis parts

   - Expected spindle runout: <0.0005" (80% improvement)

   - Expected Cp improvement: 1.15 → 1.45

2. Implement SPC with Automated Measurement ($18K)

   - Install in-process measurement probes on upgraded machines

   - Measure every part (100% vs every 10th part)

   - SPC software triggers alarm when process trends toward limits

   - Operator responds to trends before making defective parts

3. Train Operators on SPC ($3K)

   - 4-hour training for each operator (6 operators)

   - Control charts, Cp/Cpk, process adjustment strategies

   - When to adjust (special cause) vs when not to adjust (common cause)

4. Quarterly Capability Reviews ($2K annually for Aegis support)

   - Sarah visits quarterly to review capability data

   - Identify emerging issues before they become chronic

   - Share best practices across Apex's customer base

   - Total Investment:

   - Apex: $28K (spindles + measurement hardware)

   - Aegis: $28K (SPC software + training + support)

   - Total: $56K (50/50 split, similar to seal supplier model from Ch 2)

Expected Results:

   - Defect rate: 4.2% → 0.8% (80% reduction)

- Aegis saves: Inspection time, sorting, expediting, line delays
- Apex saves: Scrap reduction, improved capacity

ROI Calculation:

Current Cost to Aegis (Annual):
- Incoming inspection: 12,000 housings × 15 min × $45/hr = $135,000
- Sorting defects: 504 defects × 2 hr × $45/hr = $45,360
- Expediting replacements: 504 × $120 = $60,480
- Line delays: 504 × 4 hr × $150/hr = $302,400
- Total annual cost: **$543,240**

Cost After Improvement:
- Defect rate drops to 0.8% (96 defects/year)
- Inspection time same (still need incoming inspection)
- Sorting: 96 × 2 hr × $45/hr = $8,640
- Expediting: 96 × $120 = $11,520
- Line delays: 96 × 4 hr × $150/hr = $57,600

Total annual cost: $212,760
Annual savings: $330,480
Aegis investment: $28,000
ROI: 11.8:1
Payback: 5 weeks

Kristina presented the plan to Apex's owner, Tom Davis.

"We'll co-invest," Kristina said. "You put in $28K, we put in $28K. You get better capability, we get better quality. We both win."

Tom looked at the numbers. "Our current scrap rate on Aegis parts is 5.2%. We're catching some defects internally that don't reach you. At $180 per housing, that's $112K per year in scrap. If this drops our defect rate to 0.8%, we'll save $84K per year in scrap alone. Plus the freed-up capacity. Our payback is 4 months."

"Exactly," Kristina said. "This isn't a favor—it's an investment that benefits both of us."

Tom agreed to the plan.

Weeks 6–10: Implementation – Apex Machining

The upgrade took four weeks:
- Weeks 1–2: Spindle replacement on two machines
- Week 3: Install measurement probes and SPC software

- Week 4: Operator training, process validation

Results After Implementation:
Capability Study (New Process):
- Spindle runout: <0.0005" (was 0.002")
- Cp: 1.48 (was 1.15)
- Cpk: 1.42 (well-centered)

Defect Rate Progression:
- Baseline: 4.2%
- Week 1 after upgrade: 2.1% (spindle improvement alone)
- Week 2: 1.4% (SPC detecting drift early)
- Week 4: 0.9% (operators trained on SPC response)
- Week 8: 0.7% (process stable)

Apex Benefits:
- Scrap reduction: $84K/year
- Increased capacity: 5% (less rework)
- Customer satisfaction: Aegis increasing order volume 15%

Aegis Benefits:
- Defect rate: 4.2% → 0.7% (83% reduction)
- Savings: $330K/year
- Supply chain stability: Reliable delivery, fewer line disruptions

Month 22–24: Scaling Supplier Development

Over the next three months, Kristina and Sarah repeated the process with the other strategic suppliers.

TechBoard Electronics (Circuit Boards)
Issues:
- Solder joint quality inconsistent (3.8% defect rate)
- Manual soldering for some components
- No automated optical inspection (AOI)

Development Plan:
- Install AOI system ($45K)
- Upgrade reflow oven profile control ($22K)
- Train operators on IPC-610 standards ($5K)
- Co-investment: Aegis $36K, TechBoard $36K

Results:
- Defect rate: 3.8% → 0.6%
- ROI: 14:1

ConnectorCorp (Mil-Spec Connectors)
Issues:
- Contact resistance out of spec (5.1% defect rate)
- Crimping force variation
- No force monitoring during crimp

Development Plan:
- Install crimp force monitors on 4 presses ($28K)
- SPC on crimp force ($8K)
- Destructive test sampling increased 2× → 4× ($6K annual)
- Co-investment: Aegis $21K, ConnectorCorp $21K

Results:
- Defect rate: 5.1% → 0.9%
- ROI: 9:1

Optical Systems Inc (Lens Assemblies)
Issues:
- Focus tolerance tight (±0.003)
- Assembly fixture worn
- Environmental control inadequate (temperature swings cause thermal expansion)

Development Plan:
- New precision assembly fixture ($32K)
- Environmental controls (temp ±2°F) ($18K)
- Optical test equipment upgrade ($15K)
- Co-investment: Aegis $32.5K, Optical Systems $32.5K

Results:
- Defect rate: 2.9% → 0.5%
- ROI: 12:1

Month 24: Problematic Suppliers Develop or Replace

For the eight problematic suppliers, Kristina used a different approach.

Decision Criteria:

- If supplier is strategic (critical component, limited alternatives) → Develop
- If supplier is commodity (multiple alternates available) → Replace

Develop: ElectroPlate Services (Plating/Finishing)
- Critical capability, no local alternatives
- Issues: inconsistent coating thickness, poor process control
- Development plan: SPC on plating bath chemistry, automated thickness measurement
- Investment: $24K (50/50 split)
- Results: Defect rate 8.1% → 1.2%

Develop: Coast Castings (Aluminum Castings)
- Specialized process, long qualification time for alternatives
- Issues: porosity from inadequate degassing
- Development plan: Upgrade degassing equipment, train on vacuum casting
- Investment: $38K (50/50 split)
- Results: Defect rate 5.8% → 1.1%

Replace: Standard Fasteners, Generic Machining, ValueBoard, Industrial Coatings, BasicStamp, CheapConnectors
- Commodity parts, multiple qualified alternatives available
- High defect rates, unwilling to invest in improvement
- Action: Source alternate suppliers, transfer business over 6 months

New Suppliers (Replacements):
- Assess capability before awarding business (Cp ≥1.33 required)
- Smaller order quantities initially to validate performance
- Phased transition to minimize risk

Results:
- Replacement suppliers average defect rate: 0.6%
- Improved delivery performance: 96% on-time vs 78% from old suppliers

Month 24: Supplier Scorecard

To maintain supplier performance, Kristina implemented a simple scorecard.

Metrics (Quarterly Scorecard):

1. Quality (50% weight):
   - Defect rate (PPM parts per million defective)
   - Corrective action responsiveness
   - Capability data (Cp/Cpk) provided quarterly

2. Delivery (30% weight):
   - On-time delivery percentage
   - Lead-time consistency
   - Emergency responsiveness

3. Responsiveness (20% weight):
   - Communication quality
   - Problem-solving collaboration
   - Continuous improvement participation

Performance Tiers:
   - Platinum ($\geq$90 points): Preferred supplier, annual recognition, first priority for new business
   - Gold (80–89 points): Good supplier, maintain status
   - Silver (70–79 points): Watch list, improvement plan required
   - Bronze (<70 points): At risk, develop or replace

Quarterly Reviews:
   - Sarah meets with each strategic supplier quarterly
   - Reviews scorecard, discusses issues, identifies improvements
   - Celebrates successes (Platinum/Gold), addresses concerns (Silver/Bronze)

Year 1 Scorecard Results (After Development):
   - 4 Strategic suppliers: Platinum
   - 1 Strategic supplier: Gold (Optical Systems Inc, still improving)
   - 15 Capable suppliers: 12 Gold, 3 Silver
   - Problematic suppliers: Replaced (6), Developed to Gold (2)

Month 24: Progress Review

Twenty-four months into the transformation—exactly two years—Kristina presented results to the VP of operations and CEO.

"COPQ is down to $14M, 11.5% of revenue," Kristina reported. "That's a $16M improvement over two years."

She showed the breakdown:

COPQ Reduction Sources (Two Years):
- Design prevention (DFMEA + VOC): $8.0M
- Manufacturing prevention (Operator empowerment + poka-yoke): $6.0M
- Supplier development: $2.0M

"Supplier development was our final piece," Kristina said. "We've reduced supplier defect rate from 4.8% to 0.8%—an 83% reduction."

Supplier Development Results:

Strategic Suppliers (5 suppliers developed):
- Investment: $140K (Aegis share)
- Defect rate: 4.1% average → 0.7% average
- Annual savings: $1.4M
- ROI: 10:1

Problematic Suppliers:
- 2 developed (ElectroPlate, Coast Castings): Defect rate 7.0% → 1.1%
- 6 replaced: New supplier defect rate 0.6% average

Overall Supplier Performance:
- Total supplier defect rate: 4.8% → 0.8% (83% reduction)
- On-time delivery: 84% → 96%
- Time spent firefighting supplier issues: 240 hr/month → 45 hr/month (81% reduction)

"We're no longer spending 60% of our time sorting supplier defects," Kristina said. "Sarah and Tom can focus on prevention instead of firefighting."

The CEO asked, "What's different now versus two years ago?"

"Two years ago, we inspected quality into supplier parts," Kristina said. "If parts were bad, we sorted them and asked for replacements. Suppliers had no incentive to improve because we'd accept defects as long as they sent replacements."

"Now, suppliers build quality in. We assess their capability, invest in improvements, and hold them accountable through the scorecard. Strategic suppliers are partners—we develop them. Problematic suppliers either improve or get replaced."

She showed one more metric: "Supplier field failures."

- Year 1 (before supplier development): 47 field failures traced to supplier defects
- Year 2 (after supplier development): 8 field failures traced to supplier defects
- 83% reduction

"Supplier field failures cost $8,000 each on average," Kristina said. "We prevented 39 field failures—$312K in avoided costs."

The VP nodded. "You've essentially eliminated supplier quality as a major issue. What's next?"

"The systems we've built work," Kristina said. "But they depend on people like me championing them. We need to make prevention institutional, systems that outlast individuals. That's the next phase."

From Transaction to Partnership

Two years into the transformation, Kristina reflected on supplier relationships.

"In the beginning, suppliers were vendors. Aegis sent a PO, suppliers sent parts. If parts were bad, Aegis rejected them. If defects reached the field, Aegis charged back warranty costs. Adversarial. Transactional.

Now, strategic suppliers were partners. Aegis and Apex Machining co-invested in spindle upgrades—both benefited. TechBoard Electronics improved their AOI system—Aegis defects dropped, but so did TechBoard's other customers' defects. A rising tide lifts all boats.

The seal supplier project in Chapter 2 had proven the model worked. Precision Seals went from 3% defects to 0.6% with a $50K co-investment. ROI: 35:1.

We scaled that success to five strategic suppliers. Total investment: $140K. Total savings: $1.4M per year. ROI: 10:1.

The real change wasn't financial. It was cultural."

Tom Davis at Apex Machining had said it best: "You're the first customer who asked how they could help us improve. Usually, customers just threaten to take business elsewhere. You showed us the data, built a plan together, and invested with us. Now we're better for all our customers, not just you."

That was the shift. From "fix your quality or we'll go elsewhere" to "let's fix this together."

Suppliers weren't the enemy. They were part of the quality system. And like operators (Chapter 6), once you gave them capability, authority, and partnership, they took ownership.

Nevertheless, Kristina knew that two years of success didn't guarantee sustainability. People change. Leadership changes. Champions leave.

The next phase was about building systems that last: governance, talent development, processes that worked even when Kristina wasn't there.

Because the ultimate test of transformation wasn't what happened while she was driving it. It was what happened after she left.

Chapter 8 — The Antidote to Failure: Building a System That Learns from Every Mistake

Twenty-five months into the transformation, Kristina got the call that proves no system is perfect.

"Kristina, we have a situation." It was Jack Morrison, Program Manager for the Gen-3 infrared sensor, the one from Chapter 4 that had gone through comprehensive DFMEA. "Customer's reporting a field failure. Sensor thermal shutdown in the middle of a mission. Complete loss of function."

Kristina felt her stomach drop. The Gen-3 sensor had been flawless. Zero field failures in 18 months of deployment. 500 sensors, 36,000 operating hours, perfect record. Until now.

"Tell me what happened," Kristina said.

"Reconnaissance mission over arctic terrain," Jack said. "Sensor was operating normally, then suddenly shut down. Complete thermal runaway—housing temperature hit 195°F and triggered safety shutdown. Operator had to abort mission."

195°F? That made no sense. The Gen-3 had been designed for −40°F to +165°F housing temperature. They'd learned from the RT-4400 radio mistake and added proper margin. The thermal DFMEA had addressed overheating with a heat pipe. Validation testing had proven it worked.

"Where's the failed unit?" Kristina asked.

"Being shipped back. Should arrive tomorrow."

"Good. We're opening a CAPA. This is exactly the kind of failure we can't let happen twice."

Day 1: CAPA Initiated Discipline 1 (Form Team)

Kristina opened CAPA #2025-047 in the tracking system, the same database that had recorded 23 corrective actions for seal defects.

CAPA Title: Gen-3 Sensor Thermal Shutdown – Arctic Mission

Severity: High (mission failure, safety concern)

Customer Impact: Mission aborted, sensor unavailable for 48 hours

Occurrence: Single event (so far), but high consequence

This failure met the criteria for structured 8D problem-solving:

- High severity (mission failure)
- Customer impact (military operation disrupted)
- Successful product suddenly failing (suggests new failure mode)
- Complex system (multiple potential causes)

For simpler problems, a single defective part, obvious cause, low impact—Kristina would use lighter-weight root-cause methods. But this required full 8D.

She formed the team (Discipline 1):

Day 1 – Team Formation:

- Kristina (quality manager) – Team leader, facilitate investigation
- Mark Sullivan (design engineer) – Designed Gen-3, led DFMEA (Ch 4)
- Gary Santos (test engineer) – Validation testing, environmental qualification
- Tom Rodriguez (quality engineer) – Field failure analysis, data collection
- Captain Sarah Mills (customer representative) – User perspective, operational context

Five people, cross-functional, with a mix of design knowledge and operational experience. Small enough to be effective, large enough to have all necessary perspectives.

First team meeting scheduled for tomorrow when the failed sensor arrived.

Day 2: Problem Description Discipline 2

The failed sensor arrived in a sealed anti-static bag with a field report from the customer.

The team gathered in the lab. Kristina led them through Discipline 2: Problem Description.

"We need to describe the problem precisely," Kristina said. "Not 'sensor failed' but exactly what failed, when, where, how much."

She used the 5W+2H framework: Who, What, When, Where, Why, How, How Much.

D2 – Problem Description (5W+2H):

What: Gen-3 infrared sensor experienced thermal shutdown during operation. Housing temperature reached 195°F, triggering thermal protection circuit. Sensor became inoperative. Required power cycle to reset, but thermal shutdown recurred within 30 minutes of restart.

When:
- Date: December 15, 2025
- Time: 14:23 local time
- Operating duration before failure: 3 hours 17 minutes continuous
- Ambient conditions during failure: −28°F air temperature, direct sunlight

Where:
- Location: Arctic reconnaissance mission, northern Alaska
- Physical location: Sensor mounted on UAV gimbal, belly of aircraft
- Environmental: 15,000 feet altitude, full sun exposure

Who:
- Operator: U.S. Air Force reconnaissance unit
- Sensor: Serial number SN-502, manufactured October 2025, delivered November 2025
- Program: Gen-3 batch 5 (most recent production)

Why: Unknown (purpose of investigation)

How: Mechanism unknown, but thermal protection circuit activated at 195°F housing temperature

How Much:
- One sensor failed (out of 500 fielded)
- Mission aborted (high impact)
- Occurrence rate: 0.2% (1/500)

Captain Mills added operational context: "This was our coldest mission environment. Minus 28°F air temperature. We specifically chose Gen-3 for this mission because it's rated for arctic operations."

"Cold environment caused overheating?" Gary asked, confused.

"That's what we need to figure out," Kristina said.

Day 3: Containment – Discipline 3

Before investigating root cause, the team needed to protect the customer (Discipline 3).

D3 – Interim Containment Actions:

Immediate actions to protect customer:

1. Field Alert Issued: All Gen-3 users notified of potential thermal issue in extreme cold + sun conditions
2. Operating Restriction: Recommend limiting continuous operation to 2 hours in arctic conditions (below −20°F) until investigation complete
3. Temperature Monitoring: Request users monitor housing temperature if possible, report any temperature excursions above 160°F
4. Spare Sensor Expedited: Replacement sensor shipped to affected unit within 24 hours

Actions to prevent shipping more defects:
1. Production Hold: Gen-3 production paused (batch 5 and future batches) until root cause identified
2. Inventory Quarantine: 45 sensors in finished goods inventory quarantined, not shipped until cleared
3. Incoming Inspection Enhanced: Additional thermal testing for any sensors released from quarantine

Containment complete within 48 hours of failure report. Customer protected, production stopped, no additional defects shipped.

"Containment is temporary," Kristina told the team. "It stops the bleeding but doesn't fix the wound. Now we find root cause."

Day 4–6: Root-Cause Analysis – Discipline 4

Tom disassembled the failed sensor in the lab. The team observed.

Initial Observations:
- Thermal paste on processor heat sink had dried out, cracked
- Heat pipe showed no physical damage
- Circuit board showed heat discoloration around processor
- Housing showed no mechanical damage
- All other components appeared normal

"The thermal paste failed," Gary said. "That broke the thermal path from processor to heat pipe to housing."

"Why did the thermal paste fail?" Kristina asked. *This was 5 Whys thinking.*

5 Whys Analysis:

"Why did sensor overheat?"

→ Thermal paste dried out, breaking thermal path from processor to housing

"Why did thermal paste dry out?"

→ Thermal paste degraded in field conditions

"Why did thermal paste degrade?"

→ Unknown—need to test thermal paste response to field conditions

"Why would field conditions degrade thermal paste?"

→ Hypothesis: Temperature cycling? Altitude? Operational stress?

"Why didn't we catch this in testing?"

→ Need to compare field conditions to test conditions

The 5 Whys got them to hypotheses but not root cause. Time for deeper analysis.

Fishbone (Ishikawa) Diagram:

Kristina drew a fishbone on the whiteboard. "Let's brainstorm all possible causes, organized by category."

She drew six major bones: "Man, Machine, Method, Material, Measurement, Environment"

Man (Human Factors):

- Assembly error? (Tom checked build records—thermal paste applied correctly)
- Wrong paste amount? (SOP specifies amount, photos show correct)
- Wrong paste type? (Checked BOM—correct paste specified and used)

Machine (Equipment):
- Heat pipe defective? (Tom tested—heat pipe functional)
- Processor generating more heat than design? (Gary measured—within spec)
- Housing thermal conductivity degraded? (Tom checked—aluminum housing fine)

Method (Process):
- Thermal paste application method inadequate? (Tom reviewed—follows manufacturer guidance)
- Curing process wrong? (Thermal paste is non-curing type)

Material (Components):
- Thermal paste wrong specification? (Checked data sheet)
- Paste batch defect? (Checked batch records, other sensors in batch operating fine)

94

- Paste degradation over time? (Possible—need testing)

Measurement (Detection):
- Temperature sensor miscalibrated? (Tom tested—accurate)
- Thermal protection circuit triggered early? (Gary checked—correctly triggered at 195°F)

Environment (Operating Conditions):
- Arctic cold different from test conditions? (Gary: "We tested at −40°F")
- Altitude effect? (15,000 feet—new consideration)
- Solar radiation in cold environment? (Interesting combination)
- Thermal cycling extreme? (Cold + sun = large temperature swings)

Hypothesis Emerging: Environmental conditions in field different from test conditions in way that degraded thermal paste.

Gary pulled the test data. "We tested at −40°F chamber temperature. But we tested in lab altitude, essentially sea level. This failure was at 15,000 feet."

"Why would altitude matter?" Mark asked.

"Thermal paste contains volatile compounds," Gary said. "At high altitude, vapor pressure changes. The paste might out-gas and degrade faster."

"Combined with thermal cycling?" Tom added. "Arctic missions: sensor cold-soaked at −28°F, then direct sun exposure raises housing temperature. Sensor cycles between −20°F and +140°F multiple times per mission."

"Hypothesis Refined: Thermal paste outgassing at altitude + extreme thermal cycling (−20°F to +140°F) causes paste to dry out and crack, breaking thermal path.

"We need to test that," Kristina said.

Day 7–10: Root-Cause Validation

Gary set up validation testing: thermal paste samples subjected to altitude + thermal cycling.

Test Matrix:
1. Baseline: Thermal paste at sea level, room temperature (control)
2. Cold Only: −40°F, sea level (matches original qualification test)

3. Altitude Only: 15,000 feet equivalent, room temperature
4. Altitude + Thermal Cycling: 15,000 feet equivalent, cycle −20°F to +140°F, 50 cycles

Test Setup:
- Vacuum chamber to simulate 15,000 feet (8.5 psi vs 14.7 psi sea level)
- Thermal cycling chamber
- Thermal paste applied to test coupons (identical to production application)
- Measure thermal resistance before and after exposure

Results (10 days):

Baseline (sea level, room temp): Thermal resistance 0.24 °C/W (excellent)

Cold Only (−40°F, sea level): Thermal resistance 0.26 °C/W (acceptable)

Altitude Only (15,000 ft, room temp): Thermal resistance 0.31 °C/W (marginal)

Altitude + Thermal Cycling: Thermal resistance 1.2 °C/W (failed—thermal paste dried, cracked)

"There's the root cause," Gary said. "Altitude plus thermal cycling causes the paste to outgas volatiles and dry out. Thermal resistance increases 5×. That's enough to cause overheating."

Tom examined the failed test sample. "It looks identical to the paste in the field-failed sensor. Dried, cracked, no longer making good thermal contact."

D4 – Root Cause Identified:

Root Cause: Thermal paste specification inadequate for high-altitude + extreme thermal cycling conditions. Current paste loses volatiles at reduced atmospheric pressure, accelerated by thermal cycling between −20°F and +140°F. Thermal resistance increases 5× after 50 cycles, causing processor overheating.

Why Didn't Original Design Catch This?
- DFMEA considered thermal management but assumed sea level operations
- VOC captured temperature extremes but not altitude
- Qualification testing included −40°F but at sea level, not altitude
- Thermal cycling testing done but not at altitude

- Combined stress not evaluated (altitude + temperature + cycling together)

"This is a gap in our VOC process," Kristina noted. "We asked about temperature extremes but not altitude or combined environmental stresses. We'll fix that in D7."

Day 11–15: Corrective Action Discipline 5

Mark researched alternative thermal pastes. "We need paste that doesn't outgas at altitude and can handle thermal cycling."

He found three candidates:

1. SilverTherm XT: High-altitude rated, but expensive ($45/unit vs $8 current)
2. ArcticPro-2000: Altitude-rated, moderate cost ($18/unit)
3. MilSpec-TIM: Military specification for altitude, similar cost ($19/unit)

Gary tested all three under the altitude + thermal cycling conditions.

Test Results (After 100 cycles at 15,000 feet equivalent, −20°F to +140°F):

- SilverTherm XT: Thermal resistance 0.25 °C/W (excellent, no degradation)
- ArcticPro-2000: Thermal resistance 0.28 °C/W (good, slight degradation)
- MilSpec-TIM: Thermal resistance 0.26 °C/W (excellent, no degradation)

"MilSpec-TIM or ArcticPro-2000 both work," Gary said. "MilSpec has military pedigree, which our customer will appreciate."

D5 – Corrective Actions Selected:

For Failed Sensor (SN-502):

- Replace thermal paste with MilSpec-TIM
- Re-test at altitude + thermal cycling
- Return to customer with documentation

For Fielded Population (499 sensors):

- Issue field service bulletin (FSB)
- Retrofit thermal paste during scheduled maintenance
- Priority: Arctic-deployed sensors first (15 units), then all others over 6 months

- Cost: $19/sensor × 499 = $9,481 (material) + field service labor

For Production (Future Sensors):
  - Update BOM: Specify MilSpec-TIM thermal paste
  - Update work instruction: Application procedure (amount, surface prep)
  - Update qualification testing: Add altitude + thermal cycling test to standard qualification
  - Cost impact: +$11/sensor BOM cost

For Field Alert:
  - Once failed sensor is retrofitted and validated, lift operating restrictions
  - Confirm fix works before lifting restrictions on 499 fielded units

Day 16–20: Implementation & Validation Discipline 6

Tom retrofitted the failed sensor (SN-502) with MilSpec-TIM thermal paste.

Gary ran validation testing:
  - Altitude chamber (15,000 feet equivalent)
  - Temperature cycling (−20°F to +140°F)
  - Continuous operation (8 hours per cycle)
  - 50 cycles (simulates 1 year of arctic operations)

Results:
  - No thermal shutdowns
  - Housing temperature stable at 142°F max (well below 195°F failure threshold)
  - Thermal paste showed no degradation after 50 cycles
  - Thermal resistance remained <0.28 °C/W throughout test

"Fix validated," Gary said. "This sensor can operate in arctic altitude conditions indefinitely."

D6 – Implementation & Validation Complete:

✅ Failed sensor retrofitted, tested, validated, returned to customer

✅ Field service bulletin issued to all users

✓ Retrofit plan in progress (15 arctic sensors completed, 484 remaining)

✓ Production updated (BOM, work instructions, testing)

✓ First production unit with MilSpec-TIM completed, tested, passed

Customer feedback (Captain Mills): "Retrofitted sensor completed 12-hour arctic mission yesterday. No issues. Temperature stayed below 145°F. We're confident in the fix."

Day 21–30: Prevent Recurrence – Discipline 7

Back in Aegis, Kristina gathered the team. "We fixed this sensor. Now we prevent this from happening to other products."

D7 – Preventive Actions (Organizational Learning):

1. Update DFMEA Template

What: Add "Combined Environmental Stresses" section to DFMEA template

Why: Original Gen-3 DFMEA (Chapter 4) considered heat, cold, vibration separately but not combined effects (altitude + cold + thermal cycling)

Action: Engineering maintains DFMEA template. Mark adds new section: "Have you considered combined environmental stresses? (altitude + temperature, humidity + vibration, etc.)"

Responsibility: Mark Sullivan

Complete: Week 22

2. Enhance VOC Process

What: Add altitude and combined stress questions to VOC checklist (Chapter 5 tool)

Why: VOC captured temperature extremes (−40°F to +140°F) but missed altitude (15,000 feet)

Action: Update VOC checklist:
- "What altitude will product operate at?"
- "What combined environmental conditions occur? (cold + sun, altitude + temperature swings, humidity + vibration)"
- "Describe the most extreme mission profile—all conditions simultaneously"

Responsibility: Kristina Valdez

Complete: Week 22

3. Expand Qualification Testing Requirements

What: Add altitude testing to standard environmental qualification

Why: Current qualification tests temperature, humidity, vibration separately at sea level

Action: Test engineering updates qualification test plan:

- Altitude chamber testing (up to 20,000 feet) added to standard qualification
- Combined stress testing (altitude + thermal cycling) for products with altitude exposure
- Cost: $15K per program for altitude chamber time

Responsibility: Gary Santos
Complete: Week 23

4. Train Design Team

What: Lunch-and-learn on Gen-3 failure and lessons learned

Why: Prevent other engineers from repeating same oversight

Action: 1-hour session for all design engineers:

- Case study: Gen-3 failure (what happened, why)
- Lesson: Always consider combined environmental stresses
- Tool: Updated DFMEA template, updated VOC checklist
- Q&A: "What combined stresses might your product see?"

Responsibility: Kristina (present case study), Mark (facilitate)
Complete: Week 24

5. Update CAPA Database

What: Record lesson learned in searchable CAPA database

Why: Enable future engineers to search for similar issues

Action: CAPA #2025-047 tagged with keywords: thermal management, altitude, thermal paste, combined environmental stress, arctic operations

- If future engineer searches CAPA database for "altitude" or "thermal cycling," this CAPA appears
- Prevents relearning same lesson

Responsibility: Tom Rodriguez
Complete: Week 21

Day 35: Recognition – Discipline 8

Kristina held a team celebration.

D8 – Recognize Team:

"This investigation took 35 days from field failure to validated fix," Kristina said. "We identified a root cause that wasn't obvious, validated it with testing, implemented a fix that works, and captured lessons learned to prevent recurrence. That's textbook 8D."

She thanked each team member:

- Mark: Researched thermal paste alternatives, updated DFMEA template
- Gary: Designed validation tests, ran altitude chamber testing
- Tom: Disassembled failed unit, retrofitted with fix, updated CAPA database
- Captain Mills: Provided operational context, validated fix in field

"Most importantly," Kristina said, "we didn't hide this failure or rush a band-aid fix. We investigated properly, found root cause, and learned from it. That's how organizations build institutional memory."

She shared the results with the VP and CEO in the weekly quality review:

CAPA #2025-047 Results:

- Time from failure to root cause: 10 days
- Time from failure to validated fix: 20 days
- Time from failure to preventive actions: 30 days
- Cost of investigation + fix: $48K (testing, retrofits, field service)
- Cost avoided by preventing recurrence: $420K (estimated—prevents this failure mode on 500 existing sensors + future production)
- ROI: 8.8:1

"More importantly," Kristina added, "we updated our DFMEA template, VOC process, and qualification testing to catch this type of issue earlier in future programs. We won't repeat this mistake."

Month 27: CAPA System Maturity

Three months after the Gen-3 investigation, Kristina reviewed CAPA system performance.

The CAPA database, first mentioned in Chapter 2, with 23 corrective actions for seal defects, now contained 147 CAPAs spanning two years.

CAPA Metrics (Past 24 Months)
CAPA Volume:
- Total CAPAs opened: 147
- Average per month: 6
- Trend: Decreasing (Month 1–12: 8/month average, Month 13–24: 4/month average)

CAPA Severity:
- High severity (field failures, safety issues): 18 (12%)
- Medium severity (production defects, customer complaints): 56 (38%)
- Low severity (process improvements, audit findings): 73 (50%)

CAPA Closure Rate:
- Closed on time (<90 days): 132 (90%)
- Overdue: 8 (5%)
- Open within timeline: 7 (5%)

8D vs Simple Problem-Solving:
- 8D investigations (high severity, complex): 18 (12%)
- Simple root cause (5 Whys, obvious cause): 129 (88%)

"We don't use 8D for everything," Kristina explained to a new quality engineer. "The Gen-3 failure warranted full 8D because it was high severity, field failure, complex root cause. But most CAPAs are simpler—wrong torque wrench used, fixture worn, work instruction unclear. Those get quick 5 Whys and correction, not 35-day investigations."

Repeat Failures (Key Metric):
- Baseline (Year 1): 34 repeat failures (same root cause occurred twice or more)
- Current (Year 2): 9 repeat failures (73% reduction)

"This is organizational learning," Kristina said. "We capture lessons in the CAPA database. Engineers search it before designing. We've prevented 25 repeat failures by learning from past mistakes."

Knowledge Captured:
- Design lessons: 42 CAPAs with design root causes
- Manufacturing lessons: 68 CAPAs with process root causes
- Supplier lessons: 23 CAPAs with supplier root causes

- Testing lessons: 14 CAPAs with test/qualification gaps

"When Mark designs a new sensor," Kristina said, "he searches the CAPA database for 'thermal management' or 'altitude' or 'environmental testing.' He finds lessons learned like the Gen-3 failure. He doesn't repeat our mistakes."

Month 27: Progress Review

Twenty-seven months into the transformation, Kristina reviewed progress with leadership.

"COPQ is down to $12M, 10% of revenue," Kristina reported. "That's an $18M improvement over 27 months."

COPQ Breakdown (Current):
- Prevention costs: $2.8M (up from $600K—intentional investment)
- Appraisal costs: $1.4M (down from $1.5M—less inspection needed with better supplier/process quality)
- Internal failure: $2.6M (down from $6.9M—first pass yield improvements, operator empowerment)
- External failure: $5.2M (down from $21M—DFMEA, VOC, supplier development preventing field failures)

"The prevention investment is working," Kristina said. "We're spending $2.8M on prevention and saving $18M in failures."

She showed the CAPA system contribution:

Impact of Organizational Learning (CAPA System):
- Repeat failures reduced 73% (34 → 9 per year)
- Cost of repeat failures avoided: $1.8M/year (estimated—repeat failures are expensive because they've already failed once, require urgent fixes)
- Design lessons captured: 42 (prevents future engineers from repeating mistakes)
- Process lessons captured: 68 (prevents operators from repeating errors)

"The CAPA system is our organizational memory," Kristina said. "It prevents amnesia—forgetting what we learned from past failures."

The CEO asked, "You mentioned earlier that prevention is an investment. What's the return?"

Kristina had been waiting for this question. *It was time to show that prevention wasn't cost, it was profit.*

That conversation would happen next quarter. And it would change how leadership viewed quality forever.

Learning From Failure

Twenty-seven months into the transformation, Kristina reflected on the Gen-3 thermal failure.

Two years of prevention—DFMEA, VOC, supplier development, operator empowerment—had reduced field failures by 85%. But not to zero. The Gen-3 failure proved that no system catches everything.

The difference was how they responded.

Old response (pre-transformation): Panic. Band-aid fix. Ship replacement sensor. Hope it doesn't happen again. No investigation. No learning.

New response (post-transformation): Structured 8D investigation. Root cause validated with testing. Fix proven before implementation. Preventive actions to update DFMEA, VOC, and qualification testing. Lessons captured in CAPA database for future engineers.

Failures still happened. But now they were expensive lessons, not wasted opportunities.

The Gen-3 investigation cost $48K. But it prevented an estimated $420K in future failures by catching a systemic gap in their environmental testing approach. ROI: 8.8:1.

More importantly, it taught the organization to consider combined environmental stresses—a lesson now embedded in DFMEA templates, VOC checklists, and qualification test plans.

Failures would continue to occur. But the same failure would never occur twice. That was organizational learning.

And organizational learning, Kristina had discovered, was the difference between companies that improve and companies that don't.

The next challenge was proving to leadership that all this prevention investment—$2.8M per year—was worth it. Not just in cost avoidance but in competitive advantage.

That story started the following month.

Chapter 9 — The Quality Dividend: How Excellence Becomes a Strategic Moat

Thirty months into the transformation, Kristina sat in the CEO's office facing a question that could make or break everything.

"Kristina, I'm preparing the board presentation for next quarter," Richard Chen, the CEO, said. "The board is asking about our quality spending. They see we've increased prevention investment from $600K to $2.8M annually. They want to know: Are we getting return on this investment, or are we just spending more?"

Kristina had been expecting this question. In fact, she'd been preparing for it since the Gen-3 CAPA investigation ended (See Chapter 8).

"I can show you the return," Kristina said. "And it's not just cost avoidance. It's a competitive advantage."

Week 1: Tracking the Numbers

Kristina, Tom, and Sarah spent a week pulling together 30 months of data.

They started with the simple math: "Prevention Investment vs COPQ Reduction"

Prevention Investment (30 Months Total):
- Personnel: $1.8M (Kristina, Tom, Sarah salaries + benefits for 2.5 years)
- Training: $180K (Operator training Ch 6, DFMEA workshops Ch 4, VOC training Ch 5, 8D training Ch 8)
- Equipment/Tools: $240K (Fixtures Ch 6, error-proofing Ch 6, test equipment)
- Supplier Development: $380K (Aegis share, Ch 2 & Ch 7: seal supplier, Apex, TechBoard, ConnectorCorp, Optical Systems, plus 2 problematic suppliers)
- CAPA Investigations: $140K (Field failure investigations, testing, validation)

- DFMEA/VOC Activities: $220K (Engineering time, site visits, testing)
- Systems/Software: $80K (SPC software, CAPA database, tracking tools)

Total Prevention Investment: **$3.04M over 30 months**
COPQ Reduction:
- Baseline (Month 0): $30M (25% of $120M revenue)
- Current (Month 30): $10M (8% of $125M revenue— revenue grew slightly)
- COPQ Reduction: **$20M annually**

"Wait," the CFO would say. "You spent $3M to save $20M? That's 6.6:1 ROI. But show me where the $20M savings actually is."

Kristina had anticipated this too. She built the detailed breakdown.

COPQ Reduction by Source:

1. Internal Failure Reduction: $4.3M annually
Manufacturing Quality (Chapter 6):
- First pass yield improvement: 87% → 95%
- Rework cost reduction: $1.2M → $360K = $840K savings
- Scrap reduction: $520K → $180K = $340K savings
- Line downtime reduction: $680K → $220K = $460K savings
- Subtotal: $1.64M

Design Quality (Chapter 4):
- Prototyping rework eliminated: $880K savings (DFMEA catches issues in design, not in prototypes)
- First article failures reduced 87%: $620K savings
- Engineering change orders reduced 73%: $450K savings
- Subtotal: $1.95M

Supplier Quality (Chapter 2 & 7):
- Incoming inspection time reduced: $240K savings
- Supplier sorting/rework eliminated: $380K savings
- Expedited shipping reduced 82%: $160K savings
- Subtotal: $780K

Total Internal Failure Reduction: $4.37M

2. External Failure Reduction: $15.8M annually

Field Failures Prevented See (Chapters 4, 5, 8):
- Field failure rate: 2.1% → 0.3% (86% reduction)
- Baseline field failures: 252 per year × $8,000 average = $2.016M
- Current field failures: 36 per year × $8,000 = $288K
- Field failure cost reduction: $1.73M

Warranty Costs:
- Baseline: $2.1M annually
- Current: $420K annually
- Warranty reduction: $1.68M

Customer Credits/Penalties Avoided:
- Baseline: $1.8M (late deliveries, quality issues, penalties)
- Current: $280K
- Credits/penalties reduction: $1.52M

Premium Freight Elimination:
- Baseline: $680K (expediting to replace defective units)
- Current: $120K
- Premium freight reduction: $560K

Engineering Firefighting Reduction:
- Baseline: 40% of engineering time reactive (field fixes, customer issues)
- Current: 8% of engineering time reactive
- Value of reclaimed engineering time: $960K (engineers doing new product development instead of firefighting)

Lost Contracts Recovered/Won:
- Baseline: Lost $11M surveillance pod contract (Chapter 1) due to quality reputation
- Current: Won $18M next-gen sensor contract based on quality reputation
- Revenue impact: $18M won (not counted in COPQ savings but strategically critical)

Delayed Revenue Recovery:
- Baseline: $3M in delayed revenue due to quality issues

- Current: $400K in delayed revenue
- Cash flow improvement: $2.6M (faster time-to-revenue)

Customer Inspection Costs Eliminated:
- Baseline: $200K (customers doing perpetual source inspection due to quality concerns)
- Current: $40K (customers reduced inspection after demonstrating capability)
- Cost recovery: $160K

Repeat Failures Eliminated (Chapter 8):
- CAPA system preventing repeat failures
- Estimated cost of repeat failures: $1.8M avoided annually

Total External Failure Reduction: **$11.01M directly + $4.8M strategic** (revenue/engineering capacity)

3. Appraisal Cost Impact: Minimal Reduction ($100K)

"We didn't reduce inspection much," Kristina noted. "We still inspect suppliers and production. But inspection is catching fewer defects because defects are being prevented. Inspection cost: $1.5M → $1.4M."

The Complete ROI Picture:

Investment: $3.04M (30 months)

Annual Savings: $15.5M (Internal $4.4M + External $11.1M)

30-Month Total Savings: $38.75M (assuming linear improvement over 30 months, average $15.5M/year × 2.5 years)

ROI: 12.8:1

Payback Period: 2.3 months

"But that understates the value," Kristina told the CEO. "Because it doesn't include revenue growth from quality reputation."

Week 2: The Strategic Value

Kristina met with sales and marketing to understand the commercial impact of improved quality.

Customer Satisfaction Impact

Sales provided customer feedback data:

Customer Satisfaction Scores (NPS – Net Promoter Score):
- 30 months ago: 28 (below industry average 35)
- Current: 64 (well above industry average)
- Improvement: +36 points

Recent Customer Feedback:

"Aegis quality has improved dramatically. We're expanding our relationship." — Major defense contractor

"Field-failure rate on Aegis sensors is now lower than competitors. We're standardizing on Aegis for next-gen programs." — UAV manufacturer

"Aegis is the only supplier who proactively visits our sites to understand our requirements. Their equipment just works." — U.S. Air Force acquisition officer

Price Premium Opportunity

The VP of sales shared competitive intelligence: "Our competitors charge $1,240 for equivalent sensors. We charge $1,312, 6% premium. Two years ago, we were discounting 8% below market to win business because of quality concerns. Now we command a premium because of reliability."

Price Positioning Impact:
- Previous: 8% below market (quality concerns)
- Current: 6% above market (quality reputation)
- Net price improvement: 14%
- On $125M annual revenue: $17.5M higher revenue due to price positioning

"We're not capturing all of that," the VP of sales admitted. "But we've definitely moved from discount supplier to premium supplier. Quality is the reason."

Contract Wins Based on Quality

Sales provided examples of contracts won explicitly because of quality:

1. Next-Gen Sensor Program ($18M, 3 years):
- Competition came down to Aegis vs CompetitorX
- CompetitorX bid $16.8M (6% lower)
- Customer selected Aegis citing: "Recent quality performance, field failure rates, and supplier responsiveness"
- Quality-based win: $18M

2. Surveillance Pod Upgrade ($12M, 2 years):
- Same customer who rejected Aegis 2 years ago (Chapter 1, $11M lost contract due to quality)

- Customer: "We gave Aegis another chance based on demonstrated quality improvement. They've exceeded expectations."
- Quality recovery win: $12M

3. Arctic Sensor Program ($8M, 18 months):
- Won after Gen-3 arctic failure was fixed (See Chapter 8)
- Customer: "Aegis responded to our field failure with thorough investigation, a validated fix, and preventive actions. That's the supplier we want."
- Post-failure partnership: $8M

Total Quality-Attributed Contract Wins: **$38M over 3 years**

"These wins aren't in the COPQ calculation," Kristina told the CEO. "But they're the strategic value of quality. We're winning business we would have lost."

Week 3: The Margin Story

The CFO asked Kristina a sharp question: "Okay, you've reduced COPQ from $30M to $10M. That's $20M in cost reduction. But where did it go? Our operating margin only improved from 8% to 12%, that's $5M on $125M revenue, not $20M. Where's the other $15M?"

Kristina had the answer.

"Three places," she said. *"Growth investment, price repositioning, and volume absorption."*

1. Growth Investment ($6M)

"We reinvested $6M in new product development," Kristina said. "Engineering time that was spent firefighting (See Chapter 8, 40% reactive, now 8%) is now spent designing new products. We've launched 4 new products in the past 18 months vs 1 new product in the prior 18 months."

Engineering Capacity Freed:
- Baseline: Engineering spending 40% of time on reactive work (field failures, ECOs, firefighting)
- Current: Engineering spending 8% of time on reactive work
- Freed capacity: 32% of engineering time = $960K annually
- Invested in: New product development, technology advancement, customer-specific solutions

2. Price Positioning ($4M)

"We've moved from discount pricing to premium pricing," the VP of sales explained. "But we're phasing it in. Over the past 18 months, we've captured about $4M in improved pricing. Full price positioning will take another 12–18 months as contracts renew."

3. Volume Absorption ($5M)

"We grew revenue from $120M to $125M," the CFO noted. "That $5M in additional revenue came with very little additional overhead because we had capacity. Better quality meant less rework, which freed up production capacity for growth."

Capacity Impact:
- First pass yield 87% → 95%: Freed up 8% of production capacity
- Equivalent to adding 8% capacity without capital investment
- 8% of $120M = $9.6M capacity
- Captured $5M of that in growth, rest in reduced overtime/expediting

"So the $20M COPQ reduction split three ways," Kristina summarized:
- $5M → Operating margin improvement (visible in P&L)
- $6M → Growth investment (new products, engineering capacity)
- $4M → Price positioning (premiums vs discounts)
- $5M → Volume absorption (growth without capital)

"All four are strategic value," Kristina said. "Just not all visible as 'cost savings.'

Week 4: The Board Presentation

Kristina prepared a presentation for the board of directors. The CEO would present, but Kristina supplied the content.

SLIDE 1: The Transformation Journey

30 Months of Quality Transformation
- Starting Point: COPQ $30M (25% of revenue), field failure rate 2.1%, customer satisfaction 28 NPS
- Current State: COPQ $10M (8% of revenue), field failure rate 0.3%, customer satisfaction 64 NPS
- Investment: $3.04M over 30 months

- Return: $20M annual COPQ reduction + $38M contract wins + price premium positioning

SLIDE 2: Prevention ROI
Every Dollar Invested in Prevention Returns $12.80

Investment Category	Amount	Savings Generated	ROI
Supplier development	$380K	$2.8M annual	7.4:1
Operator empowerment	$252K	$1.64M annual	6.5:1
DFMEA/Design prevention	$220K	$1.95M annual	8.9:1
VOC/Requirements	$180K	$2.6M annual	14.4:1
CAPA/Learning system	$140K	$1.8M annual	12.9:1
Total	**$3.04M**	**$15.5M annual**	**12.8:1**

SLIDE 3: From Cost Center to Profit Driver
Quality Creates Competitive Advantage
Customer Impact:
- NPS improved 36 points (28 → 64)
- Field failures reduced 86%
- Customer willing to pay 6% premium for Aegis reliability

Revenue Impact:
- $38M in quality-attributed contract wins
- $17.5M price positioning improvement (discount → premium)
- $5M volume growth using freed capacity

Margin Impact:
- Operating margin: 8% → 12% (+$5M)
- Engineering capacity freed for growth: +$6M in new product investment

- Quality = strategic differentiator in competitive bids

SLIDE 4: What We Built
Systematic Prevention, Not Heroic Efforts
- DFMEA: All new designs, catching failures before built (Ch 4)
- VOC: Understanding customer actual needs, not assumptions (Ch 5)
- Operator Empowerment: 95% First pass yield, operators owning quality (Ch 6)
- Supplier Development: Strategic partners, 0.8% supplier defect rate (Ch 7)
- 8D/CAPA: Learning from failures, repeat failures reduced 73% (Ch 8)
- Decision Rules: Prevention required, not optional (Ch 3)
- Metrics: Quality in performance evaluations (Ch 3)

SLIDE 5: The Ask
Sustaining the Transformation
- Current prevention investment: $2.8M annually (personnel, training, development)
- Current COPQ: $10M (8% of revenue)
- Target COPQ: $8.4M (7% of revenue) within 12 months
- Request: Maintain prevention investment, continue quality as strategic priority

"The risk," Kristina wrote in the CEO's notes, "is reducing prevention investment after seeing success. That would be like stopping maintenance on a car because it's running well. Prevention must be sustained to maintain results."

Month 30: The Board Meeting

Richard Chen, the CEO, presented to the board.

"Thirty months ago, quality was a crisis," he began. "Field failures, customer complaints, lost contracts. Aegis was losing money and was at a high risk of losing our reputation."

He showed the Gen-2 sensor data. "Field-failure rate 2.4%. Customer threatening to cancel programs. We lost a $11M contract because of quality concerns."

"We invested $3 million in prevention. Here's what we got":

He showed the ROI slide: "12.8:1 return. $20M annual COPQ reduction. $38M contract wins."

"But the strategic value goes beyond numbers," he continued. "We've become the premium supplier in our market. Customers seek us out because of reliability. We're winning competitive bids based on quality, not price."

He showed customer quotes:
- "Field-failure rate now lower than competitors."
- "We're standardizing on Aegis for next-gen programs."
- "Aegis quality has improved dramatically."

"This isn't a quality initiative anymore," the CEO said. "It's our competitive strategy. Quality is how we win."

A board member asked: "What happens if we reduce quality spending to improve margins further?"

The CEO looked at Kristina in the audience. She nodded.

"We'd save $2.8M in prevention costs," the CEO said. "However, we'd lose the $15.5M in annual savings. Field failures would increase. Customers would notice. We'd go back to being a discount supplier instead of a premium supplier. That $2.8M would cost us tens of millions."

Another board member asked: "How do we know this is sustainable? What if Kristina leaves?"

"That's our next focus," the CEO said. "Building systems that outlast individuals. Making prevention institutional. That work starts next quarter."

The board voted unanimously to maintain prevention investment and recognize quality as strategic priority.

Month 30: Kristina's Reflection

After the board meeting, the CEO called Kristina into his office.

"You did it," he said. "You changed how the board views quality. They see it as competitive advantage now, not overhead."

Kristina smiled. "It was always competitive advantage. We just had to prove it with data."

"What's next?" the CEO asked.

"Sustainability," Kristina said. "We've built systems that work—DFMEA, VOC, operator empowerment, supplier development, CAPA. But they depend on people like me and Tom and Sarah to champion them. We need to make prevention institutional; systems that work even when leadership changes, when people leave, when priorities shift."

"And how do you do that?" the CEO asked.

"Governance, talent development, documentation, and rituals," Kristina said. "Make prevention so embedded in how we work that it's not an initiative, it's just how Aegis operates."

"That's critical," the CEO said. "Because in six months, our VP of operations is retiring. We're hiring a new VP from outside. I need to know your systems will survive leadership change."

Kristina felt a familiar concern. New leadership often meant "new direction"—dismantling what the previous leader built.

"That's exactly what I'll focus on," Kristina said. "Building systems that outlast people."

Quality as Strategy

Thirty months into the transformation, Kristina reflected on what had changed.

In the beginning, quality was cost. The CFO saw $30M in COPQ and asked, "How do we reduce quality spending?" The answer seemed to be: inspect less, test less, accept more defects.

Now, quality was strategy. The board saw 12.8:1 ROI on prevention investment and asked, "How do we sustain this advantage?" The answer: invest more in prevention, make quality the differentiator.

The financial case was bulletproof:
- $3M invested
- $20M annual savings
- $38M contract wins
- 12.8:1 ROI
- 86% field failure reduction
- 36-point NPS improvement

But the strategic case was more powerful:

"Aegis was no longer competing on price. They were competing on quality."

Customers paid a 6% premium because Aegis sensors worked. Competitors offered lower prices but couldn't match reliability. In critical applications—military reconnaissance, surveillance, defense, customers chose reliability over savings.

That was the transformation. From cost center to profit driver. From reactive firefighting to proactive prevention. From discount supplier to premium supplier.

The financial transformation was complete. But the organizational transformation had one more phase: making it last.

Because proving quality works for 30 months doesn't matter if it falls apart when leadership changes. Sustainability, making prevention institutional, was the final challenge.

That work started immediately.

Chapter 10 — Sustaining the Transformation: Leadership, Governance, and Talent

Thirty-one months into the transformation, Kristina got the news she'd been dreading.

The VP of operations, the one who'd backed every prevention initiative, approved the $500K prevention fund, supported decision rules, and presented quality ROI to the board, was retiring.

"I'm 67," he told Kristina. "I've been here 23 years. It's time. My last day is in three months."

"Who's replacing you?" Kristina asked.

"The CEO is hiring from outside. Someone with fresh perspective, operational excellence background, probably Six Sigma credentials. I recommended they promote internally, but the board wants outside experience."

Kristina felt her stomach tighten. New leadership from outside meant one thing: change. And change often meant dismantling what the previous leader built.

She'd seen it before at other companies. New VP arrives. "The old way worked for the old VP, but I have my own approach." Six months later, the quality systems are gone, replaced with the new VP's preferred methods. Twelve months later, quality is back to crisis mode.

"I need to make sure this high-level quality is sustained and survives after you retire," Kristina said.

"That's exactly what I was going to say," the VP replied. "You've built something great. But if it depends on me championing it, it won't last. You need to make prevention institutional."

Week 1: The Sustainability Assessment

Kristina gathered Tom and Sarah. "We have three months to make prevention bulletproof. If the new VP can dismantle what we've built, we haven't really transformed the organization."

"What are the vulnerabilities?" Tom asked.

Kristina listed them:

Vulnerability 1: Tribal Knowledge

"Too much lives in our heads," Kristina said. "How to facilitate DFMEA, how to conduct VOC site visits, how to assess suppliers, how to run 8D investigations. If Tom, Sarah, or I decide to move on, then all that knowledge leaves with us."

Vulnerability 2: Champion-Dependent

"Prevention happens because we push for it," Sarah added. "What if the new VP doesn't value it? What if they redirect us to other priorities?"

Vulnerability 3: Informal Governance

"We don't have formal governance," Tom noted. "No regular quality reviews, no prevention project tracking, no metrics dashboard. The VP knows what's happening because we talk to him weekly. A new VP might not want that kind of relationship."

Vulnerability 4: Succession Risk

"I'm the quality manager," Kristina said. "Tom and Sarah are quality engineers. But what if I get promoted or leave? Who becomes quality manager? Have we developed anyone?

Vulnerability 5: Tool Fragmentation

"Our tools are documented but scattered," Tom said. "DFMEA template in one place, VOC checklist in another, supplier scorecard in a spreadsheet, CAPA database in a different system. Not systematized."

"We have three months to fix all of this," Kristina said. "Let's build systems that outlast us."

Weeks 2–4: Documentation Making Knowledge Explicit

Kristina, Tom, and Sarah spent three weeks documenting everything.

1. *Standard Operating Procedures (SOPs)*

"SOP-001: DFMEA Process" (Chapter 4 methodology)
- When to conduct DFMEA (all new designs before release)
- How to facilitate a workshop (agenda, team composition, facilitation tips)
- Rating scales (severity, occurrence, detection with examples)
- RPN calculation and action thresholds
- Template location and usage
- Example: Gen-3 sensor DFMEA case study

"SOP-002: Voice of Customer Process" (See Chapter 5 methodology)

- When to conduct VOC (new products, new applications, new customers)
- Interview techniques (experience questions, not opinion questions)
- Site-visit checklist (what to observe, what to measure)
- Requirements translation (customer need → engineering spec)
- Use-case documentation format
- Example: RT-4400 radio VOC investigation

"SOP-003: Supplier Development" (See Chapters 2 & 7 methodology)
- Supplier segmentation (strategic/capable/problematic criteria)
- Site assessment checklist (quality system, equipment, process control, culture)
- Cp/Cpk assessment and interpretation
- Development plan structure (root cause, actions, investment, ROI)
- Co-investment negotiation guidelines
- Example: Apex Machining development

"SOP-004: 8D Problem-Solving" (See Chapter 8 methodology)
- When to use 8D vs simple problem-solving (severity criteria)
- All 8 disciplines with detailed guidance
- Root-cause tools (5 Whys, Fishbone, validation testing)
- Preventive action types (system updates, training, knowledge capture)
- CAPA database documentation requirements
- Example: Gen-3 thermal failure investigation

"SOP-005: Operator Empowerment Implementation" (See Chapter 6 methodology)
- Assessment process (observe floor, talk to operators)
- Poka-yoke design principles (prevention vs detection)
- Training curriculum structure

- Authority establishment (stop-line procedure)
- Metrics implementation (output + FPY)
- Example: Line 3 transformation

2. Templates and Tools
Quality Management System folder created with:
- DFMEA template (Excel, with rating scales and RPN calculation)
- VOC checklist (Word, with interview questions and site visit guide)
- Supplier scorecard (Excel, automated scoring)
- 8D investigation form (Word, step-by-step guide)
- Poka-yoke evaluation matrix (which type when)
- Capability study template (Cp/Cpk calculation)
- Lifecycle cost analysis template (prevention vs failure cost)

"These templates mean anyone can execute the processes," Tom said. "Not just us."

3. Training Materials
Quality Tools Training Library:
- DFMEA Facilitator Training (4-hour course, slides + exercises)
- VOC Interviewing Skills (2-hour course)
- Cp/Cpk Interpretation (1-hour course)
- 8D Problem-Solving (4-hour course)
- Poka-Yoke Design (2-hour course)
- Supplier Assessment (3-hour course)

"Now we can train new quality engineers, not just hope they learn by watching us," Sarah said.

Weeks 5–6: Governance – Making Reviews Systematic

Kristina designed simple governance structures.

Monthly Quality Review (Leadership Meeting)

Attendees: CEO, VP of operations (new VP once hired), quality manager, engineering manager, operations manager, purchasing manager

Agenda (90 minutes):

1. Metrics Dashboard Review (30 min)
   - COPQ trending (current: $10M, target: $8.4M)
   - Field-failure rate (current: 0.3%, target: 0.2%)
   - First pass yield (current: 95%, target: 96%)
   - Supplier defect rate (current: 0.8%, target: 0.6%)
   - Customer satisfaction (NPS: current 64, target: 70)

2. Prevention Project Updates (20 min)
   - Active prevention projects (status, ROI tracking)
   - Completed projects (results vs projections)
   - Upcoming projects (business cases)

3. Significant Quality Issues (20 min)
   - High-severity CAPAs (8D investigations in progress)
   - Emerging trends (new failure modes, systemic issues)
   - Customer feedback (complaints, compliments, requests)

4. System Health (10 min)
   - DFMEA completion rate (target: >90%)
   - VOC completion for new products (target: 100%)
   - Supplier assessments completed (target: all Strategic suppliers annually)
   - CAPA closure rate (target: >90% within 90 days)

5. Decisions & Actions (10 min)
   - Resource needs
   - Policy changes
   - Strategic quality priorities

Documentation: Meeting minutes with decisions and action items, distributed within 24 hours

"This meeting makes quality visible to leadership," Kristina explained. "Every month, they see the data. They can't ignore it. And it happens whether I'm here or not—the meeting is on the calendar."

Quarterly Prevention Project Review (Working Meeting)

Attendees: Quality team, engineering, operations, purchasing representatives

Purpose: Deep-dive on prevention investments and returns

Agenda (2 hours):

1. Prevention investment YTD (spending by category)

2. COPQ reduction (actual vs projected)
3. ROI by project (which investments delivered best returns)
4. Lessons learned (what worked, what didn't)
5. Next quarter priorities (which problems to tackle)

"This is where we track whether prevention is paying off," Tom said. "We show the data quarterly. If ROI drops, we adjust. If it's strong, we keep investing."

Weekly Quality Team Huddle (Internal)
Attendees: Kristina, Tom, Sarah (Quality team only)
Purpose: Coordination and problem-solving
Agenda (30 minutes):
- Week's priorities

- Issues blocking progress

- Help needed from leadership

- Skill development (learning from each other)

"This keeps us aligned," Sarah said. "But it's just coordination, not governance."

Weeks 7–8: Talent Development – Building Bench Strength

Kristina focused on developing people who could sustain the transformation.

Tom's Development (Succession Planning)
"Tom, in twelve months, you'll be ready to be quality manager," Kristina said.

Tom looked surprised. "You're leaving?"

"I don't know," Kristina said honestly. "But whether I leave or not, you need to be ready. If I get hit by a bus, the transformation shouldn't collapse."

Tom's Development Plan:
- Lead Monthly Quality Reviews: Tom presents metrics starting next month (Kristina observes, coaches)

- Facilitate Two DFMEA Workshops: Tom leads, Kristina observes

- Conduct One Supplier Assessment: Tom leads Apex annual review

- Present at Board: Tom presents prevention ROI next quarter (practice for leadership communication)

- Strategic Planning: Tom participates in annual quality strategy planning

"You know the technical work," Kristina said. "You need practice leading, presenting to executives, and thinking strategically."

Sarah's Development (Technical Depth)

Sarah, you're the supplier development expert," Kristina said. "I want you to train others."

Sarah's Development Plan:
- Train Two Operations Engineers: Teach Cp/Cpk assessment and capability studies
- *Mentor New Quality Engineer*: Aegis was hiring a third QE—Sarah would mentor them
- Document Best Practices: Sarah writes "Supplier Development Playbook" based on Chapters 2 & 7 work
- Present at Industry Conference: Sarah submits paper on supplier co-investment model

"You're becoming the thought leader on supplier development," Kristina said. "That expertise needs to spread."

Operator Quality Coaches

Kristina worked with operations to develop operator quality coaches.

"Line 3 transformation succeeded because operators took ownership," Kristina told the operations manager. "What if we trained operators to teach quality to other lines?"

They selected three operators from Line 3:
- "James" (Station 2—the first to stop the line)
- "Angela" (Station 5—suggested improvements)
- "Carlos" (Station 4—proposed color-coding)

Quality Coach Training:
- What makes quality good? (technical standards)
- How to spot problems (inspection techniques)
- When to stop the line (authority and procedure)
- How to suggest improvements (poka-yoke thinking)
- How to teach peers (coaching skills)

"James, Angela, and Carlos will help implement operator empowerment on Lines 8, 9, and 10 next quarter," the operations manager said. "They'll teach what they learned."

"That's how culture scales," Kristina said. "Peer to peer, not top-down."

Weeks 9–10: Rituals Embedding Culture Through Repetition

Kristina established recurring activities that reinforced prevention culture.

Weekly Floor Walks (Leadership Visibility)

"Every Tuesday, 8:00 AM, VP operations + quality manager walk the floor"

- Visit one production line per week
- Talk to operators: "What problems are you seeing?"
- Observe processes: "Is the poka-yoke working?"
- Check metrics boards: "Is first pass yield trending up?"
- Thank operators who stopped the line: "Good catch last week, Maria."

"This isn't an inspection," Kristina explained to the VP. "It's showing operators that leadership cares about quality. When they see you asking about problems, they know it's safe to report them."

The VP agreed to maintain the floor walks. "Whoever replaces me needs to do this too. It's how leadership stays connected."

Monthly Lunch-and-Learns (Knowledge Sharing)

"Last Friday of each month, noon–1:00 PM, open to all employees"

- Rotating topics: DFMEA basics, Cp/Cpk explained, 8D case studies, poka-yoke examples
- Presenters: Quality team, engineers, operators, suppliers
- Recent topics: "How Apex Machining Improved Capability" (Tom Davis, supplier), "Line 3 Transformation Story" (James, operator), "Gen-3 Arctic Failure Investigation" (Mark Sullivan, engineer)

"These sessions share knowledge across the company," Tom said. "New employees learn prevention mindset. Veterans share experiences."

Quarterly Prevention Showcases (Celebrating Success)

"First Friday of quarter, 2:00 PM, all-hands meeting."
- Quality team presents quarter's prevention wins
- Teams present their projects (operators, engineers, suppliers)
- CEO recognizes high-performing teams
- Metrics shown: COPQ reduction, field failures prevented, contract wins

"This celebrates prevention," Sarah said. "It makes quality visible. People see that preventing problems gets recognized."

Annual Quality Day (Cultural Event)

"We should make quality an event," Kristina proposed. "One day per year, focused on quality."

Annual Quality Day (planned for Month 36):
- Morning: CEO keynote on quality as competitive advantage
- Workshops: DFMEA training, poka-yoke design, supplier development
- Poster session: Teams present prevention projects
- Awards: Best prevention project, operator quality champion, supplier partner of year
- Afternoon: Site tours for customers (show them the quality systems)

"This makes quality a celebration, not a chore," Kristina said.

Weeks 11–12: The New VP Arrives

The new VP of operations arrived in Month 33.

Jennifer Martinez had twenty years of operational experience—automotive manufacturing, Six Sigma Black Belt, led turnarounds at two companies. Resume was impressive. But Kristina was nervous.

"Tell me about the quality transformation," Jennifer said in her first week.

Kristina walked Jennifer through the journey:
- Starting point: $30M COPQ, 2.1% field failures, lost contracts
- Prevention investment (30+ months): $3M in prevention, systematic approach

- Current state: $10M COPQ, 0.3% field failures, 12.8:1 ROI, premium supplier
- Systems built: DFMEA, VOC, operator empowerment, supplier development, CAPA/8D

Jennifer asked sharp questions:
- "What's preventing COPQ from going lower?" (Resource constraints, diminishing returns on some initiatives)
- "How do you know prevention is sustainable?" (Governance, documentation, talent development)
- "What if I want to change the approach?" (Show me data that your approach works better)

Kristina respected the skepticism. Jennifer wasn't accepting things blindly. She was testing.

"Come to the Monthly Quality Review next week," Kristina said. "See the data. Meet the team. Then decide if you want to change anything."

Month 33: The Quality Review Test

Jennifer attended her first Monthly Quality Review.
Kristina presented the dashboard:
COPQ Trending:
- Month 0: $30M (25%)
- Month 33: $9.5M (7.6%)
- Target: $8.4M (7%)

On track to hit target in 3 months
Field Failures:
- Current: 0.3% (36 failures per year out of 12,000 deliveries)
- Target: 0.2%
- Trending: Declining

First Pass Yield:
- Current: 95% across all lines
- Target: 96%
- Line 3: 96% (leading indicator)

Supplier Quality:
- Defect rate: 0.8%
- On-time delivery: 96%

- Strategic suppliers: All Platinum/Gold on scorecard

Customer Satisfaction:
- NPS: 64 (industry-leading)
- Recent feedback: 3 customers increased order volumes citing quality

Tom presented prevention project ROI:
- Q1 projects: $180K invested, $2.2M annual savings, 12:1 ROI
- Examples: Line 8 poka-yoke, connector stress relief, thermal validation expansion

Sarah presented supplier development:
- Optical Systems Inc capability improvement: Defect rate 2.9% → 0.5%
- ROI: 12:1 on $32.5K investment

Mark Sullivan (guest) presented DFMEA impact:
- Four new products launched in past year
- Zero field failures on DFMEA-designed products (vs eight field failures on legacy products)
- DFMEA completion rate: 94%

Jennifer asked: "What's your biggest concern?"

"Sustainability," Kristina said. "We've built systems that work. But they require ongoing investment—personnel, training, and prevention spending. If the company cuts prevention investment to boost short-term margins, we'll regress. That's what happened at previous companies I've worked at."

"Show me the data if we cut prevention," Jennifer said.

Kristina pulled up sensitivity analysis:

Scenario A: Maintain Prevention Investment ($2.8M/year)
- COPQ: $9.5M → $8.4M (target achieved)
- Field failures: 0.3% → 0.2%
- Customer satisfaction: 64 → 70 NPS
- Projected revenue impact: +$15M over 3 years (contract wins, price premium)

Scenario B: Cut Prevention Investment 50% ($1.4M/year)
- Personnel: Reduce from 3 QEs to 2 QEs (lose Sarah or Tom)

- Supplier development: Stop co-investments, revert to reactive supplier management
- Training: Eliminate operator training, DFMEA workshops
- Impact (modeled):
- COPQ: Stabilizes at $12M (regresses $2.5M)
- Field failures: Increase to 0.6% (doubled)
- Supplier defects: Increase to 2.5% (3× increase)
- Customer satisfaction: Declines to 50 NPS
- Lost revenue: −$8M over 3 years (customer defections, price pressure)

Net: Save $1.4M/year in prevention, lose $2.5M/year in COPQ + $8M in revenue = $10M worse over 3 years

Jennifer studied the analysis. "So, cutting prevention costs more than maintaining it."

"Exactly," Kristina said. *"Prevention looks like cost until you stop doing it. Then you see it was an investment."*

Jennifer nodded. "I'm not touching your budget. Show me what you need to get COPQ to 7%."

Month 34–36: Final Push to 7% COPQ

With Jennifer's support, Kristina executed the final improvements.

Remaining COPQ Sources ($9.5M → $8.4M target, $1.1M reduction needed):

1. Legacy Product Quality Issues ($400K opportunity)

Products designed before DFMEA implementation still generating field failures.

Action: Retrospective DFMEA on top 3 legacy products
- Identify failure modes in current designs
- Implement design changes in next production run
- Expected reduction: 15 field failures/year × $8K = $120K
- Plus warranty reduction: $280K

2. Inspection Inefficiency ($300K opportunity)

Still inspecting at same frequency despite improved supplier/process quality.

Action: Risk-based inspection
- Strategic suppliers with Platinum rating: Reduce from 100% to sampling

128

- Capable processes (Cp >1.67): Reduce inspection frequency
- Resources redirected to prevention activities
- Expected reduction: $300K inspection labor

3. Prototyping Waste ($200K opportunity)
Some prototyping rework still occurring on complex assemblies.
Action: Expand design validation testing
- Add virtual validation (simulation before hardware)
- Increase design reviews (catch issues earlier)
- Expected reduction: $200K prototyping rework

4. Small Supplier Issues ($200K opportunity)
Fifteen capable suppliers occasionally generating defects.
Action: Preventive supplier assessments
- Annual capability reviews
- Early intervention before defects occur
- Expected reduction: $200K sorting/rework

Total Expected Reduction: $1.1M → Target $8.4M COPQ achieved
By Month 36, COPQ reached $8.4M (7% of revenue).

Month 36: Systems Proven

Three years into the transformation—exactly 36 months from when Kristina mapped COPQ, she reviewed progress with Jennifer.
"COPQ is at $8.4M, 7% of revenue," Kristina reported. "That's a $21.6M improvement over three years."
"What's the three-year ROI?" Jennifer asked.
Kristina had all the numbers ready to present:
Three-Year Investment:
- Prevention spending: $3.4M
- Personnel (Kristina, Tom, Sarah): $2.2M
- Total: $5.6M

Three-Year Savings:
- COPQ reduction: $21.6M annually (cumulative $32M over 3 years with gradual improvement)
- Contract wins: $38M (quality-attributed revenue)
- Price premium: $17.5M potential (phased in)
- Total value: $87.5M
- ROI: 15.6:1 over three years

"And the systems are institutional now," Kristina said. "They don't depend on me."

She showed the evidence:

Documentation:

- Five SOPs covering all major quality processes
- Fifteen templates and tools ready to use
- Training library (seven courses, all documented)

Governance:

- Monthly Quality Review (16 consecutive meetings, never missed)
- Quarterly Prevention Review (12 consecutive reviews, ROI tracked)
- Weekly floor walks (CEO + VP, 52 weeks straight)
- Monthly lunch-and-learns (24 sessions, avg 45 attendees)

Talent:

- Tom promoted to senior quality engineer, ready for quality manager role
- Sarah recognized as supplier development expert, mentoring new QE
- Three operator quality coaches trained and deployed
- Knowledge transfer complete

Rituals:

- Quality reviews calendared for next two years
- Floor walks established routine
- Lunch-and-learns scheduled through next year
- Annual Quality Day planned for next month

"If I left tomorrow," Kristina said, "Tom could run this. The systems would continue. The governance would keep quality visible. The talent is developed. The rituals would sustain the culture."

Jennifer then asked the critical question: "Do you believe that? Really?"

Kristina paused. "Six months ago, I would have said no. The transformation was me. Now? Yes. Tom can do my job. Sarah can develop suppliers. The operators are quality owners. The engineers do DFMEA automatically. The systems work."

"Good," Jennifer said. "Because I need to talk to you about something."

Month 36: The Offer

Jennifer closed the door to her office.

"The CEO and I have been talking," Jennifer said. "Aegis is growing. We're opening a second facility in Arizona—$200M revenue when fully operational. It'll have 6 production lines, 600 employees, same aerospace work we do here."

Kristina listened.

"We need someone to set up the quality function there. Build it from scratch. Implement everything you've built here—DFMEA, VOC, supplier development, operator empowerment, the whole system. But in a greenfield facility."

"You want me to move to Arizona?" Kristina asked.

"We want you to be director of quality for the new facility," Jennifer said. "Bigger role, bigger budget, more impact. And you'd build it right from day one instead of transforming a broken system."

Kristina felt conflicting emotions. Excitement—building from scratch would be amazing. Fear—leaving what she'd built. Pride—they trusted her to do it again.

"What about here?" Kristina asked. "Who becomes quality manager?"

"Tom," Jennifer said. "He's ready. You've trained him. The systems are documented. He'll be fine."

"Can I think about it?"

"Take two weeks," Jennifer said. "Kristina—this is a big promotion. You've earned it."

Built to Last

Thirty-six months into the transformation, Kristina reflected on what she'd built.

The quality systems worked. COPQ at 7%. Field failures at 0.2%. Customer satisfaction at 67 NPS. Premium supplier. $87.5M value created over three years.

But the real measure wasn't the numbers. It was whether the systems could survive without her.

Three years ago, she'd been the hero—the one person fighting for quality. If she'd left in Month 6, the transformation would have died.

Now, the transformation was institutional:

- DFMEA happened because it was required (Chapter 3 decision rules), not because Kristina pushed for it
- VOC happened because engineers knew customers rewarded it (Chapter 5 + 9 contract wins), not because Kristina mandated it
- Operators owned quality because metrics rewarded it (Chapter 3 + 6 FPY), not because Kristina convinced them
- Suppliers developed capability because scorecards tracked it (Chapter 7), not because Kristina visited them
- 8D investigations happened because CAPA system required them (Chapter 8), not because Kristina led them

The systems didn't need her anymore. They were documented. Governed. Staffed with trained people. Reinforced through rituals. Measured through reviews.

Tom could be quality manager. Sarah could develop suppliers. The operators could teach peers. The engineers could facilitate DFMEA. Jennifer could lead quality reviews.

Kristina had built something that didn't need her. That was the ultimate success.

The Arizona opportunity was exciting. Building a quality system from scratch—implementing everything she'd learned—would be the next challenge.

But first, she had one more thing to do. Make sure the transition to Tom was seamless. Ensure the systems continued. Prove the transformation was truly sustainable.

That final proof would come in the next chapter. When Kristina leaves, will the systems survive?

Chapter 11 — The Legacy: Building an Organization That Outlasts You

Thirty-seven months into the transformation, Kristina made the hardest decision of her career.

She accepted the promotion.

Director of quality, Aegis Arizona facility. Greenfield operation. Building a quality system from scratch. Everything she'd learned over three years—DFMEA, VOC, operator empowerment, supplier development, 8D, governance, rituals—implemented from day one.

It was the opportunity of a lifetime. But it meant leaving what she'd built.

Month 37: The Transition

Kristina spent two months helping Tom transition into the role.

Weeks 1–2: Shadowing

Tom shadowed Kristina for two weeks—every meeting, every decision, every interaction.

In the monthly quality review, Tom presented the dashboard while Kristina observed. Jennifer (VP of operations) asked questions. Tom answered confidently:

- "COPQ is 7.1%, trending toward 7% target."
- "Field failures are 0.2%, lowest in company history."
- "Two prevention projects in progress: Line 9 poka-yoke and thermal validation expansion."

After the meeting, Jennifer pulled Kristina aside. "He's ready."

Supplier Site Visit: Tom and Sarah visited TechBoard Electronics for their annual assessment. Kristina came along but stayed quiet. Tom led the assessment—reviewed capability data, walked the floor, discussed improvement opportunities. The TechBoard quality manager said afterward, "Tom knows this stuff as well as you do."

DFMEA Workshop: Tom facilitated a DFMEA workshop for a new radar housing. Kristina sat in the back. Tom guided the team through functions, failure modes, ratings, actions. The team didn't look to Kristina once—they followed Tom's lead.

"You don't need me anymore," Kristina told Tom after the workshop.

"I haven't needed you for the past six months," Tom said with a smile. "But it's nice having you around."

Weeks 3–4: Handoffs

Kristina handed off all her responsibilities.

Strategic Relationships:

- Introduced Tom to CEO: "Tom is my successor. Trust him like you trust me."
- Introduced Tom to key customers: "Tom will be your quality contact. He knows our systems better than anyone."
- Introduced Tom to strategic suppliers: "Tom has been part of every supplier development project. He'll continue what we started."

Knowledge Transfer:

- Reviewed all SOPs together (Chapter 10 documentation paying off)
- Walked through governance calendar (reviews scheduled for next year)
- Discussed talent development (Sarah mentoring new QE, operator coaches scaling)
- Shared lessons learned ("Watch out for complacency. Prevention requires constant vigilance.")

Final Quality Review:

Kristina presented her last monthly quality review—not as quality manager, but as a retrospective.

"Thirty-nine months ago, I walked into this company and saw a quality crisis," Kristina began. She showed the Chapter 1 data:

- COPQ: $30M (25% of revenue)
- Field failures: 2.1%
- Customer satisfaction: 28 NPS
- Lost $11M contract due to quality reputation
- Quality was firefighting, not prevention

"Today, we're a different company," she continued. She showed current data:

- COPQ: $8.5M (7% of revenue)—$21.5M improvement

- Field failures: 0.2%—90% reduction
- Customer satisfaction: 67 NPS—39 point improvement
- Won $38M in contracts based on quality reputation
- Quality is prevention, not firefighting

"But the numbers don't tell the full story," Kristina said. "The story is how we got here."

She clicked through the journey:

The Wake-Up Call: Mapped COPQ, found $30M hidden across the company, got $500K prevention fund approved, started with seal supplier.

First Proof Point: Seal supplier project, 35:1 ROI, proved prevention worked, established co-investment model.

Making Prevention Default: Decision rules ("No design released without DFMEA"), metrics alignment (output + quality, not just output), prevention became required not optional.

Preventing Design Failures: DFMEA on Gen-3 sensor, caught four high-risk issues before production, zero field failures, 12:1 ROI on design changes.

Understanding Real Requirements: RT-4400 radio failure, VOC site visit to Fort Bragg, learned actual use differs from specification, requirement failures reduced 73%.

Operators Owning Quality: Line 3 transformation, first pass yield 89% → 96%, operators empowered to stop line, poka-yoke preventing defects, quality became everyone's job.

Suppliers as Partners: Five strategic suppliers developed, supplier defect rate 4.8% → 0.8%, co-investment model scaled, suppliers became partners not vendors.

Learning from Failures: Gen-3 arctic failure, complete 8D investigation, root cause validated, preventive actions updated systems, repeat failures reduced 73%.

Quality as Strategy: Proved 15.6:1 ROI to board, won $38M contracts based on quality, moved from discount to premium supplier, quality became competitive advantage.

Building to Last: Documented all processes, created governance, developed Tom and Sarah, established rituals, made prevention institutional not personal.

"And now," Kristina said, "I'm leaving. Not because the work is done—continuous improvement never ends. But because the systems don't need me anymore. Tom will be your quality manager.

He's ready. The systems are documented. The governance is in place. The talent is developed. The culture is embedded."

She looked at Tom. "This transformation was never about me. It was about building something that outlasts any individual. Tom, it's yours now."

The room applauded. Several people were emotional—Kristina had been the face of quality transformation for three years.

But Kristina felt peace. She'd built something that would survive her departure. That was the ultimate success.

Month 39: Kristina Leaves

Kristina's last day at Aegis was bittersweet.

She walked the floor one final time, stopping at Line 3—where operator empowerment had started.

James was at Station 2, the operator who'd pressed the stop button that first time.

"Hey James," Kristina said. "Remember when you first stopped the line?"

James laughed. "I was terrified. Thought I'd get in trouble."

"You changed the culture that day," Kristina said. "You showed everyone it was safe to stop for quality. Now it's normal."

"It's just how we work now," James said. "New operators come in, we teach them: you see a problem, you stop the line. Nobody thinks twice about it."

That was it. "Just how we work now." Not an initiative. Not a program. Just culture.

Kristina visited Sarah, who was training the new quality engineer on supplier assessments.

"You're the supplier development expert now," Kristina told Sarah. "Keep building those partnerships."

"I learned from the best," Sarah said. "The seal supplier project taught me everything—site assessment, Cp/Cpk, co-investment, building trust. I've used that model twenty times now."

Kristina visited Tom in what was now his office.

"You've got this," Kristina said.

"I know," Tom said. "You trained me well. But I'm still going to miss having you here."

"Call me anytime," Kristina said. "But you won't need to. You know the systems, you know the people, you know the data. You're ready."

"What's your first priority in Arizona?" Tom asked.

"Show them the iceberg" Kristina said with a smile. "Map COPQ, show leadership the hidden costs, get prevention budget approved, find the seal supplier equivalent. Start the cycle again."

"Three years from now, they'll be where we are now," Tom said.

"That's the plan," Kristina said. "And maybe I'll train my successor there too. Build it, make it sustainable, move on. That's the model."

She walked out of Aegis for the last time. Three years of her life invested in this transformation. But it was complete. The systems worked. The culture had changed. Tom was ready.

Time to do it again in Arizona.

FLASH FORWARD: Two Years Later

Kristina was in her office in Arizona—now 18 months into building the quality system at the new facility—when her phone rang.

"Tom! How are you?"

"Great," Tom said. "Just finished our monthly quality review. Thought you'd want to hear the numbers."

"Always," Kristina said.

"COPQ is at 6.8%," Tom reported. "We've been at 7% for two years, but we just implemented risk-based inspection and that saved another $200K. Field failures are at 0.18%—we haven't had a high-severity CAPA in eight months. Customer NPS is 71, highest in company history."

Kristina felt proud. "You didn't just sustain—you improved."

"We ran the numbers," Tom continued. "Since you left two years ago, we've reduced COPQ another $700K. Four-year total improvement is now $22.2M. ROI on the original prevention investment is now 18:1."

"What's driving the continued improvement?" Kristina asked.

"The systems you built," Tom said. "DFMEA catches design issues. VOC captures real requirements. Operators own quality. Suppliers are partners. 8D prevents repeat failures. The governance keeps it visible. The rituals keep it reinforced. It's all still working."

"And the people?" Kristina asked.

"Sarah got promoted to senior quality engineer," Tom said. "She's running supplier development for the whole company now— both facilities. She's training your Arizona team next month."

"I heard, that's fantastic," Kristina said.

"We hired two more quality engineers," Tom continued. "Both joined in the past year. I'm training them the way you trained me— SOPs for technical skills, shadowing for leadership skills, practice for confidence."

"Are they getting it?" Kristina asked.

"One of them asked me last week who created the DFMEA template," Tom said. "I told her you did, when we were transforming Gen-3 sensor. She said, 'Who's Kristina?' She'd only been here six months. Didn't know who you were."

Kristina laughed. "That's perfect."

"I told her," Tom said, "'Kristina Valdez was the quality manager who taught us that prevention is cheaper than firefighting. She built all the systems we use—DFMEA, VOC, supplier development, 8D, governance. Then she left because the systems didn't need her anymore.'"

"What did she say?" Kristina asked.

"She said, 'Wow. These systems are so good, I thought they'd been here forever.'"

Kristina felt a swell of emotion. That was the ultimate compliment. The systems were so embedded, new employees thought they'd always existed. Prevention was "just how we do things."

"That's the legacy," Kristina said. "When the transformation becomes invisible because it's just normal."

"There's more," Tom said. "Remember that $11M surveillance pod contract we lost? The customer who rejected us because of quality issues?"

"Of course," Kristina said. "That was the wake-up call."

"They just awarded us a $24M next-generation surveillance pod contract," Tom said. "Three-year program. They said, and I quote, 'Aegis quality transformation over the past four years has been remarkable. Field-failure rates, customer responsiveness, and partnership approach make Aegis our preferred supplier for critical systems.'"

Kristina was speechless. Full circle. The contract they'd lost because of poor quality—now won back because of excellent quality.

"We calculated the total value of quality transformation," Tom continued. "Four years in, we're at $22M COPQ reduction annually, plus $65M in quality-attributed contract wins, plus $22M in price premium positioning. Total value: $109M. Original investment: $6.2M. ROI: 17.5:1."

"Quality isn't overhead," Kristina said, echoing the board presentation. "It's profit."

"Exactly," Tom said. "The board increased our prevention budget last quarter. They see quality as strategic investment, not cost. Jennifer (VP of operations) told the CEO, 'Quality is the foundation of everything we do. We don't cut the foundation.'"

"How's Jennifer doing?" Kristina asked.

"She's a quality champion now," Tom said. "Does floor walks every Tuesday, just like the old VP did (Chapter 10 ritual). She asks operators about problems, thanks people who stop the line, reinforces prevention culture. She gets it."

"Leadership continuity," Kristina said. "That's what makes sustainability real."

"One more thing," Tom said. "We're hosting a quality conference next month—'Manufacturing Quality Excellence Forum.' Sarah is presenting on supplier co-investment. I'm presenting on operator empowerment. Mark Sullivan is presenting on DFMEA. We have 200 attendees registered from other aerospace companies. Aegis is now the thought leader on quality transformation."

Kristina smiled. "You've taken what we built and made it even better. That's exactly what should happen."

"We're standing on your shoulders," Tom said. "You laid the foundation. We're building on it."

"No," Kristina said. "You're standing on your own feet now. The transformation was never about me. It was about systems, culture, and people like you carrying it forward."

The Cultural Transformation: What Success Looks Like

After hanging up with Tom, Kristina reflected on what defined successful transformation.

It wasn't the COPQ numbers, though $22M in annual savings was impressive.

It wasn't the ROI, though 17.5:1 was extraordinary.

It wasn't the contract wins, though $65M in quality-attributed revenue proved strategic value.

The transformation was complete when these things happened:

1. *New Employees Think Systems Are Normal*

New quality engineer didn't know who Kristina was. Assumed DFMEA, VOC, supplier development, 8D were "just how Aegis does things." Prevention wasn't an initiative—it was culture.

2. *Systems Continue Improving Without Original Champion*

Tom reduced COPQ another $700K after Kristina left. Sarah scaled supplier development to second facility. Engineers improved DFMEA template. Operators refined poka-yoke. Continuous improvement happened organically, not because champion pushed it.

3. *Leadership Changes Don't Disrupt Systems*

VP of operations retired (Chapter 10), new VP hired, systems continued. Jennifer adopted floor walks, supported prevention investment, reinforced culture. Leadership transition tested and passed.

4. *People Say "This Is Just How We Work"*

James (operator): "Just how we work now." Not "the quality initiative" or "Kristina's program"—just normal. Engineers automatically schedule DFMEA. Purchasing automatically assesses suppliers. Operators automatically stop for quality. Default behavior changed.

5. *Transformation Becomes Thought Leadership*

Aegis hosting conference, presenting at industry forums, other companies learning from them. Moved from "quality crisis" (Chapter 1) to "quality excellence example" (Chapter 11). Transformation proved and scalable.

6. *Original Champion Moves On*

Kristina accepted the promotion, and left Aegis. She started her career transformation again in Arizona. Could only leave because systems didn't need her. If transformation required her presence, she'd be trapped. Freedom to leave proved sustainability.

7. *Metrics Sustain and Improve*

COPQ: $30M → $8.5M (4 years) → $8.1M (Year 5) → continuing downward. Field failures: 2.1% → 0.2% → 0.18%. Customer satisfaction: 28 → 67 → 71. Not plateau—continuous improvement.

8. *Next Generation Carries Forward*

Tom training two new QEs. Sarah mentoring Arizona team. Operator coaches teaching new lines. Knowledge transfer happening peer-to-peer. Second generation of quality champions emerging. Sustainability proven through succession.

"Arizona: The Cycle Repeats"

Kristina looked at her Arizona metrics dashboard.

"Arizona Facility Quality Transformation (18 months in):
   -   COPQ: Started at $48M (24% of $200M revenue)

   -   Current: $32M (16% of revenue)

   -   Field failures: Started at 3.2%, current 1.1%

   -   Customer NPS: Started at 35, current 52

"We're on the same trajectory," Kristina thought. "Following the same playbook."

"Arizona (Months 1–3): Mapped COPQ, got $800K Prevention Fund, started with circuit board supplier (the Arizona equivalent of Precision Seals from original Chapter 2).

"*Arizona (Months 4–9)*: Proof point (circuit board supplier, 28:1 ROI), decision rules implemented, metrics aligned.

"*Arizona (Months 10–18)*: DFMEA on all new designs, VOC for new aerospace customer, operator empowerment on Lines 1–2.

"Three years from now," Kristina told her Arizona team in a recent all-hands meeting, "you'll be where Aegis was when I left. 7% COPQ, 0.2% field failures, 70+ NPS, quality as competitive advantage. And when I leave to start this somewhere else, you'll continue improving. Because I'm not building Kristina's quality system—I'm building your quality system."

Her team was nodding. They got it. This wasn't about her. It was about systems that worked.

The Phone Call: Five Years Later (Month 99)

Five years after Kristina first mapped COPQ at Aegis, she got another call from Tom.

"Kristina! Big news."

"What's up?"

"Aegis just won the largest contract in company history," Tom said. "$180M, five-year program, next-generation multi-domain surveillance system. Customer is U.S. Department of Defense. Competitive bid against three major defense contractors."

"Congratulations!" Kristina said. "That's incredible."

"The customer selection report cited quality as the primary decision factor," Tom continued. "They said, 'Aegis demonstrated consistent quality performance over five years. Field-failure rates 87% lower than industry average. Customer satisfaction scores consistently exceed benchmarks. Quality systems and processes are mature and validated. Aegis is the low-risk choice for mission-critical systems.'"

Kristina felt goosebumps. Five years ago, quality was why Aegis lost contracts (Chapter 1: $11M surveillance pod rejected). Now, quality was why Aegis just won the largest contract in company history.

"Quality went from liability to competitive advantage," Kristina said.

"Completely," Tom agreed. "The board presentation last quarter showed the five-year financial impact. COPQ reduction: $120M cumulative. Quality-attributed contract wins: $267M cumulative. Price premium positioning: $38M cumulative. Total value created: $425M. Original investment: $8M over five years. ROI: 53:1."

"That's transformation," Kristina said. "Fifty-three to one."

"The CEO told the board," Tom continued, "'Quality transformation was the single best investment Aegis ever made. We're a different company now. Quality is who we are, not just what we do.'"

"How's the culture?" Kristina asked.

"Sarah just promoted to quality irector—she oversees quality for both facilities now," Tom said. "The two quality engineers I hired four years ago are now senior QEs—one leads DFMEA for the company, the other leads supplier development. We hired three new QEs last year. I'm training them the same way you trained me."

"And you?" Kristina asked.

"I got offered VP of quality," Tom said. "Company wants to expand to a third facility on the East Coast. They want me to oversee quality for all three facilities."

"That's fantastic," Kristina said. "Are you taking it?"

"I am," Tom said. "But I'm promoting Sarah to quality manager here before I move. She's ready. Same succession model you taught me—build the person, document the systems, create governance, establish rituals, make it sustainable, move on."

"The cycle continues," Kristina said.

"We're teaching what you taught us," Tom said. "Build prevention systems that outlast the builder. That's the legacy."

Epilogue: The Legacy (Ten Years Later)

Ten years after Kristina first walked into Aegis and saw $30M in COPQ, she attended an aerospace quality conference.

She was now VP of quality for a Fortune 500 aerospace company—the culmination of a 20-year career. But she still remembered where the transformation journey started.

At the conference, a young quality engineer approached her during the break.

"Excuse me, are you Kristina Valdez?"

"I am," Kristina said.

"I work at Aegis Aviation," the young engineer said. "I joined three years ago. I've been using your quality systems—DFMEA template, VOC checklist, supplier development playbook, 8D process. They're all documented in our SOPs. I wanted to say thank you. These tools work."

Kristina smiled. "You're welcome. But those aren't my systems anymore. They're Aegis' systems. You and your team own them now."

"Tom Rodriguez—our VP of quality—he told us you built all of this," the young engineer said. "Back in 2025. It's 2035 now. Ten years later, and everything you built is still working. Actually, it's even better. We've improved the templates, refined the processes, adapted to new technologies. But the foundation you laid—

prevention over firefighting, systems over heroics, culture over programs—that's still core to who we are."

"How's Aegis doing?" Kristina asked.

"COPQ is at 5.2%," the engineer said. "Field failures are at 0.08%. We just won a $300M contract based on quality reputation. Our customer NPS is 78. We're the benchmark for aerospace quality."

"And Tom?" Kristina asked.

"He's amazing," the engineer said. "He teaches us the same way you taught him. He says, 'My job is to build quality engineers who are better than me, just like Kristina built me to be better than her.' He's training his successor right now—our current quality manager, Sarah Chen."

Kristina laughed. "Sarah Chen. I hired Sarah fresh out of college ten years ago. Now she's quality manager. That's what succession looks like."

"Tom tells us stories from the transformation," the engineer continued. "The seal supplier project with 35:1 ROI. The Gen-3 sensor DFMEA that prevented field failures. The RT-4400 radio VOC investigation in Fort Bragg. The Line 3 operator empowerment. The Gen-3 arctic failure 8D investigation. The board presentation proving quality ROI. Those stories are part of Aegis culture now. New employees learn them in quality orientation."

"Those weren't just stories," Kristina said. "They were the transformation. Each one taught us that prevention works, that data matters, that people are the solution, that quality is strategy."

"They're inspiring," the engineer said. "They show us that quality isn't boring compliance work—it's competitive advantage. We're not preventing defects because someone tells us to. We're preventing defects because that's how we win."

"That's the culture shift," Kristina said. "When prevention becomes identity, not initiative. When people say, 'This is who we are,' not 'This is what we do.'"

"Thank you for starting that," the engineer said. "Your legacy lives on."

After the engineer left, Kristina reflected on the word "legacy."

Legacy wasn't the COPQ numbers, though $30M → $5.2M over ten years was remarkable.

Legacy wasn't the ROI, though 53:1 return proved financial value.

Legacy wasn't the contracts won, though $267M in quality-attributed revenue demonstrated strategic impact.

Legacy was culture. Systems that outlasted the champion. People carrying forward the mindset. New generations learning from old stories and building on them.

Legacy was a young engineer, ten years later, using tools she'd created, improved by people she'd trained, in a company that didn't need her anymore.

That was success. Building something that doesn't need you. Teaching people who teach others. Creating systems that improve after you leave.

Quality transformation wasn't about Kristina. It never was.

It was about showing people that prevention works, giving them tools that prove it, building systems that sustain it, and stepping aside so they could carry it forward.

That was the legacy.

Appendices

Supporting resources to enhance your quality transformation journey

Appendix A: Glossary of Quality Terms

This glossary provides definitions for key terms and acronyms used throughout the book.

8D — Eight Disciplines of Problem-Solving — A structured method for root-cause analysis and corrective action

A3 — A problem-solving methodology documented on a single A3-sized piece of paper, emphasizing visual management

Andon — A visual or auditory signal system that alerts when a problem occurs, empowering workers to stop production

APQP — Advanced Product Quality Planning — A structured framework for product development from concept through production

AS9100 — Aerospace quality management system standard based on ISO 9001 with additional requirements

Blameless Investigation — Root-cause analysis that focuses on systemic issues rather than individual fault

CAPA — Corrective and Preventive Action — Systematic approach to eliminating root causes and preventing recurrence

COPQ — Cost of Poor Quality — Total cost of failures, prevention, and appraisal activities

Cp — Process Capability Index — Ratio of specification width to process variation (assumes centered process)

Cpk — Process Capability Index (adjusted) — Accounts for process centering between specification limits

CTQ — Critical to Quality — Key measurable characteristics that significantly impact customer satisfaction

DFMEA — Design Failure Mode and Effects Analysis — Systematic evaluation of potential design failures

DFM/DFA — Design for Manufacturability / Design for Assembly — Design practices that ease production

ECN — Engineering Change Notice — Formal documentation of design or process changes

FAI — First Article Inspection — Comprehensive inspection of initial production units (AS9102)

FPY — First Pass Yield — Percentage of units passing all inspections without rework

Gemba — Japanese term meaning "the real place" — going to where work happens to observe and learn

IATF 16949 — Automotive quality management system standard

IPT — Integrated Product Team — Cross-functional team responsible for product development

IQ/OQ/PQ — Installation/Operational/Performance Qualification — Equipment validation protocol

ISO 9001 — International standard for quality management systems

ISO 13485 — Quality management standard for medical devices

Kaizen — Continuous improvement philosophy emphasizing small, incremental changes

MSA — Measurement Systems Analysis — Evaluation of measurement system accuracy and precision

MTBF — Mean Time Between Failures — Average time between failures in a repairable system

MTTR — Mean Time To Repair — Average time required to restore functionality after failure

OTIF — On-Time In-Full — Delivery performance metric

PDCA — Plan-Do-Check-Act — Iterative four-step management method for continuous improvement

PFMEA — Process Failure Mode and Effects Analysis — Systematic evaluation of potential manufacturing failures

PLM — Product Lifecycle Management — Software system managing product data from concept through disposal

Poka-Yoke — Error-proofing devices or techniques that prevent mistakes

PPAP — Production Part Approval Process — Automotive industry standard for part approval

PPM — Parts Per Million — Defect rate measurement (defective parts per million opportunities)

QMS — Quality Management System — Formalized system documenting processes and responsibilities

RCA — Root-Cause Analysis — Systematic investigation to identify fundamental causes of problems

ROI — Return on Investment — Financial metric measuring gain relative to cost

ROP — Return on Prevention — ROI specific to prevention investments

RPN — Risk Priority Number — FMEA scoring: Severity × Occurrence × Detection

SPC — Statistical Process Control — Using statistical methods to monitor and control processes

VOC — Voice of Customer — Systematic gathering and translation of customer requirements

Appendix B: Template & Tool Library

A comprehensive index of all templates, calculators, and frameworks referenced in the book. Access the complete library at dign2quality.com/tools

Financial & Strategic Planning
Quality P&L Template — Chapter 1
COPQ Calculator — Chapter 1
Lifecycle Cost Model Framework — Chapter 2
Prevention ROI Calculator — Chapter 2
Quality Dividend Financial Model — Chapter 9
Executive Quality Scorecard — Chapter 9

Product Development & Design
APQP Phase Checklist — Chapter 4
DFMEA Template — Chapter 4
PFMEA Template — Chapter 4
Control Plan Template — Chapter 4
Design Review Checklist — Chapter 4
Tolerance Stack Analysis Worksheet — Chapter 4

Measurement & Statistical Tools
MSA Gage R&R Calculator — Chapter 4
Cp/Cpk Calculator — Chapter 4
SPC Control Chart Templates — Chapter 4
Process Capability Study Guide — Chapter 4

Customer & Requirements
Customer Ecosystem Mapping Template — Chapter 5
Ethnographic Observation Guide — Chapter 5
CTQ Scorecard — Chapter 5
VOC Interview Template — Chapter 5
Field Maintenance Checklist — Chapter 5

Organizational & Cultural
Organizational Design Assessment — Chapter 3
Decision Rights Matrix — Chapter 3
Quality Council Charter — Chapter 3
Andon System Design Guide — Chapter 6
Psychological Safety Survey — Chapter 6
Near-Miss Reporting Form — Chapter 6

Supplier Management
Supplier Segmentation Matrix — Chapter 7
Supplier Capability Qualification Checklist — Chapter 7
Supplier Scorecard Template — Chapter 7
Supplier Audit Guide — Chapter 7
Co-Investment Contract Clauses — Chapter 7
Supplier Development Playbook — Chapter 7

Incident & CAPA Management
Incident Response Playbook — Chapter 8
RCA Toolkit (5 Whys, Fishbone, Fault Tree) — Chapter 8
CAPA Tracking Template — Chapter 8
Blameless Investigation Checklist — Chapter 8
Lessons Learned Template — Chapter 8

Industry-Specific Tools
AS9102C FAI Tool (Aerospace) — Available at dign2quality.com
PPAP Package Generator (Automotive) — Available at dign2quality.com
IQ/OQ/PQ Suite (Pharma/Medical) — Available at dign2quality.com
QMS Audit Checklist (ISO 9001/AS9100/IATF) — Available at dign2quality.com

Governance & Sustainability
CQO Charter Template — Chapter 10
Quality Investment Board Operating Procedures — Chapter 10
Competency Framework Template — Chapter 10
Balanced Scorecard Template — Chapter 10
Succession Planning Template — Chapter 11
Knowledge Codification Checklist — Chapter 11

Appendix C: Quality Standards & Certifications Reference

Key quality management standards and certification programs relevant to manufacturing excellence.

ISO 9001:2015

Scope: Quality Management Systems — Requirements

Application: Universal quality management standard applicable to all industries

Key Focus: Process approach, risk-based thinking, leadership commitment

AS9100D

Scope: Quality Management Systems — Aerospace

Application: Based on ISO 9001 with additional aerospace-specific requirements

Key Focus: Configuration management, FOD prevention, critical items control

IATF 16949:2016

Scope: Quality Management Systems — Automotive

Application: Automotive industry quality standard

Key Focus: APQP, PPAP, MSA, SPC, zero defects mentality

ISO 13485:2016

Scope: Quality Management Systems — Medical Devices

Application: Medical device manufacturers and suppliers

Key Focus: Risk management, design controls, traceability

AS9102C

Scope: First Article Inspection Requirement

Application: Aerospace first article inspection and documentation

Key Focus: Complete characteristic accountability, Forms 1–3

AIAG APQP

Scope: Advanced Product Quality Planning

Application: Automotive product development framework

Key Focus: Five-phase product development process

AIAG PPAP

Scope: Production Part Approval Process

Application: Automotive supplier part approval

Key Focus: 18-element submission package, 5 submission levels

AIAG FMEA-4

Scope: Failure Mode and Effects Analysis

Application: DFMEA and PFMEA methodology

Key Focus: Seven-step approach, action priority

Appendix D: Recommended Reading & Resources

Essential books, articles, and resources to deepen your quality management knowledge.

Foundational Quality Books

Out of the Crisis by W. Edwards Deming — Classic text on quality management philosophy and systems thinking

The Goal by Eliyahu M. Goldratt — Theory of constraints applied to manufacturing

Quality Is Free by Philip B. Crosby — Business case for quality and zero defects

Juran's Quality Handbook by Joseph M. Juran — Comprehensive quality engineering reference

The Toyota Way by Jeffrey K. Liker — Lean manufacturing and continuous improvement culture

Practical Implementation Guides

The ASQ Certified Quality Engineer Handbook by ASQ Quality Press — Technical reference for quality practitioners

APQP Reference Manual by AIAG — Official automotive APQP standard

FMEA-4 Manual by AIAG & VDA — Harmonized DFMEA and PFMEA methodology

Statistical Quality Control Handbook by Western Electric — Classic SPC reference

Measurement Systems Analysis (MSA) by AIAG — Official MSA standard and procedures

Organizational & Cultural

High Output Management by Andrew S. Grove — Leadership and organizational design

The Fearless Organization by Amy C. Edmondson — Psychological safety in the workplace

Turn the Ship Around! by L. David Marquet — Leader-leader model and empowerment

The Fifth Discipline by Peter M. Senge — Learning organizations and systems thinking

Industry Standards Bodies & Resources

ASQ (American Society for Quality) — www.asq.org — Certifications, training, publications

AIAG (Automotive Industry Action Group) — www.aiag.org — Automotive quality standards

SAE International — www.sae.org — Aerospace and automotive standards

ISO (International Organization for Standardization) — www.iso.org — International standards

IAQG (International Aerospace Quality Group) — www.iaqg.org — Aerospace quality standards

Online Communities & Forums

Dign2Quality Community — dign2quality.com/community

ASQ Quality Progress Magazine — Quality trends and case studies

iSixSigma Forums — Lean Six Sigma discussions

Manufacturing Leadership Council — Industry networking

LinkedIn Quality Management Groups — Peer networking

www.ingramcontent.com/pod-product-compliance
Lightning Source LLC
Chambersburg PA
CBHW060514290526
45791CB00001B/379